I dedicate this book to the Lord Jesus,
the One who forgives and teaches us how to forgive;

And to my elegant children, Madison, Morgan, Unathi and
Nkosi Mackenzie Chamu Jr.:
May you grow in the forgiveness of God.

CONTENTS

We All Need Forgiveness

When you live long enough or you love hard enough, you are going to experience pain at some point in your life. You will be hurt by the actions of others, or sometimes you will be hurt by your own, wrong decisions. That means that at some point you are also going to need to forgive. You may even have a relationship that falls apart—whether it is because someone hurt you or you hurt someone else—and you will seek reconciliation. You will do this because God calls us to forgive as well as to obey. Since you love God, you will want to do as He commands. Therefore, you need to gain an understanding of what these words mean in a biblical context, and how you can have the power to live them out.

In the life of a believer, the cross paints a picture of forgiveness and reconciliation. It makes it possible for us to be forgiven, to forgive, and to be reconciled with God and with our brothers and sisters. Even though the cross makes forgiveness possible, that doesn't mean it is easy. There is vulnerability that comes when we forgive, but there is grace available to do all that God has called us to do—and that includes forgiving.

Each of us has a God-given purpose on this earth. Joy and fulfillment come from living out that purpose. God's perfect plan is for us to live in harmony together, but we live in a fallen world, which means that in the process of living out our purpose we are sometimes hurt, or we sometimes hurt others. When we hold on to the pain, we take the focus off of God, which can hinder His forgiveness and blessing. Equally destructive is allowing people back into our lives, believing that forgiveness is the same as reconciliation. Both of these attitudes open the door to Satan and his plans.

I encourage you to have your Bible beside you as you read, so that you can study the verses with me and allow God to speak to your heart through this time of study. Workbook sections with questions and action steps at the end of each chapter will help you delve further into the principles of forgiveness, reconciliation, and restoration explored in this book.

As you read this book, you will learn why we forgive, how to forgive, and the benefits of forgiveness. You will also learn what forgiveness is not, how it has been used by the enemy to keep you in bondage, and how God seeks to set you free by forgiving. Although it can be hard to forgive, this book will show you how God has equipped you to do all the things that God calls you to do in His Word.

CHAPTER ONE

Why Forgive?

Forgiveness is hard!

At times, it can feel like forgiveness costs more than it's worth. Despite this, throughout His Word, God calls us to forgive. Jesus set the example for the New Testament believer on the cross when He asked God to forgive those who were participating in His crucifixion (Luke 23:34).

We may understand that we are called to forgive, but do we really understand why? Do we really understand what it means to forgive? How do we respond when we apologize to someone and the person doesn't accept our apology? These are all important questions in the life of a believer, because when we don't obey God's commands—among them the call to forgive—we find ourselves living in bondage and not living the life God intended for us to enjoy.

To begin the lesson on forgiveness, we must first define the key terms. *Forgiveness* and *reconciliation* seem to be used interchangeably in our culture, but from a biblical perspective they are quite different. For our purposes, forgiveness is about the decisions of one person, but reconciliation involves the decisions of two people. To clarify this further, I can forgive someone who wrongs me, but it requires his or her participation for us to reconcile.

Forgiveness, as we will learn about it in this book, can involve other people or just us. By that I mean that we sometimes need to forgive others, and sometimes we need to forgive ourselves. However, this can be difficult, because there is emotional energy that comes with the anger or conviction that we've been wronged by someone else. Furthermore, being angry at ourselves can motivate us to try harder or to push further. It causes us to put up protective emotional walls that insulate us from hurt caused by others. There are a variety of reasons we use to justify not forgiving someone.

1. If you forgive, then the offender might think what he or she did didn't hurt you that much.

2. You believe the first one to give in is the weak one, and you don't want to be seen as weak.

3. If you forgive, then the offender wins and goes on with his or her life.

4. You have been burned once and refuse to let anyone do that to you again. Unfortunately, people who feel this way sometimes punish the whole world and not just the offender.

5. You think the offender only deserves punishment, not forgiveness.

6. You are willing to forgive, but not until the offender shows remorse.

7. You deny forgiveness because you don't believe the offender's apology was genuine.

8. The offender has not asked for forgiveness.

9. The other person blames you and has demanded that you forgive him or her.

When you look at these reasons, it seems that most people choose not to forgive because they feel that it will hurt less if they don't forgive. However, the consequences of unforgiveness are actually quite painful. Let's look at some of those now.

Unforgiveness: Reasons and Consequences

There are many consequences to our emotions, spiritual health, and even our physical bodies when we choose not to forgive. Many individuals are sick with diseases because of an unforgiving spirit. The Bible says that a merry heart is like medicine (Proverbs 17:22 NKJV). Instead of taking medicine to get past your tension headache, choose to forgive. Bitterness has a way of changing who you are, just as forgiveness can.

Unforgiveness, anger, and bitterness are like secondhand smoke. When you harbor these sentiments, you hurt those around you as well as yourself. That is because bitterness cannot produce anything positive, no matter how much you pray when you are bitter.

When you forgive, you benefit, the person you forgive benefits, and God benefits. By contrast, when you allow bitterness to take root because you refuse to forgive, many people can become defiled. How many people are being affected right now because you are bitter? How much trouble are you dealing with in your life right now because you are holding on to an offense? Who are you so angry at right now that you are willing to spoil how your life story ends?

As a counselor, I've met some people who have become bitter because someone broke their hearts. Bitterness is contagious. Have you ever gone to lunch with someone who is bitter? You'll leave that place bitter yourself. Have you ever had somebody give you a call and tell you something bad about someone else, and then you started spreading it? You are now spreading that bitterness.

So, I want to challenge you: Everybody knows somebody who is struggling with bitterness and unforgiveness. God cannot forgive you if you don't forgive others (Matthew 6:14–15). You tie the hands of God when you don't forgive others.

See, unforgiveness has a way of contaminating everything around it, much like a dirty pipe that carries water. If there is something wrong with the pipe, it contaminates everything that flows through it. When you don't forgive, it taints everything that comes through you and through your life. It affects how you deal with people, including your own children. It also affects how you view God.

When you refuse to forgive, you are the person who suffers. The other person is still living his or her life and probably doesn't even realize you're angry. God calls us to let it go because He knows the destruction of unforgiveness in our bodies and in the corporate body of Christ. See, unforgiveness does not deliver on its promise to hurt the other person, but it is consuming you.

Not only that, but also consider the impact on children raised in families in which parents are angry at each other.

Lack of forgiveness is a cancer that destroys from the inside out. You cannot hold another person down without staying down with that person, as well. Likewise, you cannot be beautiful with unforgiveness in your heart. It's been said that unforgiveness is like drinking a bottle of poison and hoping somebody else dies.[1]

Have you ever been around people who are unhappy? How did it make you feel? Unforgiveness grows if it goes unchecked. I have counseled people who are in their fourth or fifth marriages because they're still not addressing issues that occurred in their first marriage. They're trying to change faces instead of dealing with the root cause of their problems. It will never work, because when you don't forgive, you put yourself in bondage. It becomes a roadblock that prevents you from moving forward. You cannot go forward personally, spiritually, or relationally when you refuse to forgive.

Look at Romans 3:10: "There is none righteous, no, not one" (NKJV).

When we refuse to forgive other people, we make up justifications, but this verse says that all of us make mistakes and have done things requiring forgiveness. If we want to be forgiven, we also need to learn to forgive. We see that in the Lord's Prayer, where Jesus said to ask for forgiveness from God "as" we forgive others (Matthew 6:12 NKJV). That means "in the same way." Is that what we really want? To be held to the same standard to which we hold others?

While you consider that, let's move on to the next section and look at God's mandate of forgiveness.

Biblical Mandate for Forgiveness

Forgiveness is a command. As with all other commands, we forgive in order to obey God. We forgive because we have been forgiven. When I don't forgive, I'm denying that I've been forgiven. When forgiveness seems difficult, remember that we are not forgiving because of the other person and what the person did, but because of God and what He did.

Because we want to obey God, we want to bring glory to Him and join His team for reconciliation. You're living for God, not looking at the flesh. You forgive others as you've been forgiven, and if you don't, you're denying what you know God did for you.

We forgive in order to delight in God. Don't look at all of the blessings in your life for your glory. You are not blessed for you; you are blessed for His glory. God is in the business of sharing. While most people keep the best things for themselves, God gives the best things He has, then calls us to do the same.

God tells us to give, and He promises we will get it back (Luke 6:38). Why does He do this? Because when we give, we do what He does and we've brought attention to Him. So, when we give forgiveness, it is a delight to God.

> *By this we know love, that he laid down his life for us, and we ought to lay down our lives for the brothers.*
> *—1 John 3:16 (ESV)*

> *For God so loved the world that he gave his one and only Son, that whoever believes in him shall not perish but have eternal life.*
> *—John 3:16 (NIV)*

In other words, heaven is about sharing the best that heaven has. When you forgive, you forgive to bring glory to God. It may benefit the human being, but your goal is God's glory. Didn't Jesus say that "whoever believes in me will do the works I have been doing, and they will do even greater things than these" (John 14:12 NIV)?

When you choose to forgive, you help assist the possibility of God's mission of reconciliation. Second Corinthians 5:17–19 has this to say: "Therefore, if anyone is in Christ, the new creation has come: The old has gone, the new is here! All this is from God, who reconciled us to himself through Christ and gave us the ministry of reconciliation: that God was reconciling the world to himself in Christ, not counting people's sins against them. And he has committed to us the message of reconciliation" (NIV).

Look at that. Through Christ, God was reconciling the world to Himself, not counting people's trespasses against them, and He has committed to us the word of reconciliation. When we forgive, God reconciles.

"We are therefore Christ's ambassadors, as though God were making his appeal through us. We implore you on Christ's behalf: Be reconciled to God" (2 Corinthians 5:20 NIV).

If you want to be a part of something great, start forgiving. When you forgive, it is as if you are letting God deal with that person through you. God wants us to be a divine extension of who He is, in such a powerful way that it is as if the people in question were in His very presence. God wants us to forgive and reconcile as if we are God Himself. We are to be God's hands and feet on earth, but when you forgive another person, you are God's heart on earth. When you forgive, you take part in God's greatest mission.

When you fully understand the meaning and power of forgiveness and reconciliation, you will be excited. Everyone has been hurt. Jesus was hurt. However, He still calls us to forgive and reconcile. He'll bear the scars of the hurt throughout eternal ages, but rather than reminding us of our sin, those scars now remind us of His intense love for us. It is a love strong enough to break the powers of sin, the devil, and the grave (Romans 6:10 NLT). Jesus died to give us freedom.

Forgiveness is freedom. Unforgiveness brings bondage. If you want to experience freedom, then you must forgive.

Forgiveness must become a lifestyle. Don't hold on to anger and hurt when someone wrongs you (Ephesians 4:26). Take your focus off of the hurt and drop the issue. Ask God to take it and release that person entirely. That is what a lifestyle of forgiveness is all about. Focus on the good things God has done *for you* rather than the wrong someone else has done *to you*.

Whatever you focus on, you empower. You don't get better by remembering what hurts you the most, but rather you empower it. However, if you focus on being free, you will become free.

This explains why some people are so blessed, but they are still not happy. When you are holding on to sins of the past, you relive the pain continually. Sometimes the hurt continues even after the other person has died. You may never get an apology from the other person, but you still must release the power of the event, attitude, or behavior over your life. Rather than making you weak, forgiveness makes you strong, because you are creative, healthy, and free. You are capable of moving on to the next thing God has for you.

Abraham Lincoln said he would rather turn an enemy into a friend.[2] That's what God has done with us. We were all enemies of God, but through Jesus Christ He made us His friends (Romans 5:10 NIV). That's what forgiveness does. We may not eat together again, but we are free not to wish each other to choke.

Pray this prayer with me:

Father, thank You for what You've done. There are many emotions that have been awakened, because forgiveness is not something we can do on our own. You have to enable us, and the Holy Spirit has to empower us to let it go. We're here to interact with the Word of God. We've heard the command of God that we must do what Christ did. So, God, help us release the bitterness of unforgiveness. Lift our burden away. Amen.

WORKBOOK

Chapter One Questions

Question: What are some of the consequences of unforgiveness and some of the blessings of forgiveness?

_____

_____

_____

_____

_____

_____

_____

_____

_____

_____

_____

Question: Why do people choose bitterness over forgiveness? How does bitterness affect those around the bitter person?

_____

_____

_____

_____

_____

_____

_____

_____

_____

_____

_____

Question: How does forgiveness bring glory to God? Write down an example of someone who helped others reconcile with God by choosing to forgive.

_____

_____

_____

_____

_____

_____

_____

_____

_____

_____

_____

Action: Journal about a time when you needed forgiveness. What was your offense, and how did the
offended party respond? Did they choose to forgive you?
Was there reconciliation?

_____

_____

_____

_____

_____

_____

_____

_____

_____

_____

_____

_____

_____

Chapter One Notes

CHAPTER TWO

Forgiveness: A Choice

In the Bible, God is not embarrassed to share the things people would most want to hide. Have you noticed that? God exposed the fact that Peter denied Jesus three times (Matthew 26:69–75). He freely describes the fall of great men like Moses, Abraham, Gideon, and David. He shows the misplaced enthusiasm of Peter and Saul. But He also shows the strength that comes through obedience in the cases of individuals like Boaz or Mary. The Bible shows the impact of the good and bad choices each of us makes.

When I was growing up as a young man in the church, I really struggled with the difference I saw between the brokenness of my heroes in the Bible and the outward perfection of the people in the pews with me. While David cried out from the depths of his soul for forgiveness when he sinned (Psalm 51:1–12), I didn't see others testifying about their struggles with addictions and temptations. Furthermore, the people who did show their struggles were punished by the church—not helped.

That eventually led me to wonder why the Bible exposes the things most people try to cover up. Have you ever considered why this is?

The Bible shows this not to expose the wrong, but to expose the underlying relationship problem. This is a crucial distinction. We find stories in the Bible of people committing wrongdoing, because forgiveness can only occur where there was a wrong. There can only be reconciliation when a relationship has been shattered. So, God ensured the story of Cain (Genesis 4) was included in the Bible so we could see how committing murder affects a person's relationship with other people and with God. Learning about the consequences of wrong actions leads us to greater appreciation of the heart of forgiveness.

Jesus taught about forgiveness through the parable of the unmerciful servant in Matthew 18:21–35. Jesus told the story of a man who came to settle his accounts. "The kingdom of heaven is like a certain king who wanted to settle accounts with his servants" (Matthew 18:23 NIV). You may know the story: The king called a man in who owed him ten thousand talents, but the man couldn't pay. The debt was too great. Therefore, the king commanded that everything the man owned and all of his family be taken as payment. The servant begged for mercy and promised to repay the king. Even though this king knew it was impossible for the man to repay, he forgave the debt.

Once forgiven, the very same man walked out of the presence of the king and soon encountered a man who owed him a very small amount: one hundred denarii. The same man who had just been forgiven the large debt commanded that this man with a small debt be thrown into prison until he repaid his entire debt.

Understand the impact of unforgiveness on our emotions and thinking. This person was interested in getting the small amount of money back, but he put the other man in jail, a location from where the other man clearly cannot repay his debt. This makes it obvious that the first man didn't want repayment; he wanted control.

Think about your own bitterness. Do you bring up the hurt and offense? Do you want control over that person and his or her actions because of emotional manipulation? Do you want to release the person and forgive, or do you want to control the person through your anger?

Look back at the story that Jesus told. Someone witnessed what the forgiven man had done and went back to the king to tell him what happened.

The forgiven man was called back into the king's presence, and the king became angry.

> Then the master called the servant in. "You wicked servant," he said, "I canceled all that debt of yours because you begged me to. Shouldn't you have had mercy on your fellow servant just as I had on you?" In anger his master handed him over to the jailers to be tortured, until he should pay back all he owed.
>
> This is how my heavenly Father will treat each of you unless you forgive your brother or sister from your heart.
> —*Matthew 18:32–35* (NIV)

The story is not about what happened. The story is about not sharing what you yourself have received. God has forgiven every single sin you've ever committed. It was an insurmountable debt that you could never have made up for. When you don't forgive, you withhold grace from another person. People only grow in the context of grace, so if you are not willing to extend it, nothing will ever change.

Forgiveness is first a choice, and then an action. You can never forgive by accident. It may also hurt you to forgive somebody, but you have to be determined to give somebody a second chance. God says that we don't forgive people because they deserve it; we forgive people because He forgave us when we didn't deserve it (Ephesians 4:32; Colossians 3:13; Romans 5:8). God is counting on us to do for others the supernatural thing that He did for us. So now let's look at how we forgive, because it is more than simply saying, "It is okay" if someone apologizes.

Authentic Forgiveness

So, what does it really mean to forgive? You've seen in this book the benefits of forgiveness and how God clearly tells us to forgive, but, in our culture, the idea of what forgiveness is can become confusing. True forgiveness is something that happens on the inside and then becomes clear on the outside. Here are some characteristics of authentic forgiveness:

You release the right to retaliate. When you authentically forgive, you choose not to get even. You give up your right to hit back. If it still hurts when you think about the person who hurt you, it means you haven't forgiven that person. There are many people who do well as long as they avoid the person who hurt them. That doesn't mean they've shown forgiveness. It means they still have to deal with the offense.

You know you have authentically forgiven when you no longer define the offender by the offense. That's why, when you read your whole Bible, Jesus never called anyone a sinner. He called us "the lost." Once you call someone a sinner, you're defining that person by his or her sin.

God never defines you by what you have done. With God, there's always hope. He always talks to you about what you are becoming—not what you are struggling with.

When speaking to others, speak to them in terms of what you see them becoming, not who they currently are. When Gideon was hiding out and sifting his grain, the angel came to him and called him a "mighty warrior" (Judges 6:12 NIV). Nothing about him at that moment was either mighty or like a warrior, but God spoke the future into Gideon's present.

When you're able to look at that person who hurt you and call him or her a brother or sister in Christ (or some other kind term), you know that you are healing from your wound. As long as you define the individual as "the person who did X to me," you haven't yet released the offense.

People cannot hurt you without the enemy's help. Anyone who is hurting you is also struggling and is being abused by the enemy. That means you both have a common enemy. The Bible tells us that we wrestle not against flesh and blood, but against principalities, powers, and spiritual wickedness in high places (Ephesians 6:12 KJV). When we forgive people, then we allow God's healing and love to shine through us to that person. We allow God to reach past us to them. While you may feel that you don't want that person to experience God's healing touch, the truth is, you do. You are going to be an agent of God or the devil in this world, so which would you prefer? When you forgive, you become God's agent for change. Do you really want the alternative?

The whole world was moved after the South Carolina church shooting, when people went to court and forgave the shooter.[3]

The people of that community said, "You know what? You killed people we loved during a Bible study, but we just want you to know that we're praying for you to find Jesus." Think of the impact of that. Think of how God can work through that to make something beautiful out of a horrible situation.

By contrast, some people who have divorced, when they hear that their former spouse is about to get married to someone else, they have sleepless nights simply because they haven't fully released that person. You need to get to a point in your walk with God where you wish all people well, because even the person who hurt you deserves good things from the Lord, too.

The funny thing about it is that God loves the person who hurt you the same way He loves you.

There is a command to forgive. While I've spent a great deal of time telling you all of the benefits of forgiveness—and there are many—one very important reason to forgive is simply because God told us to. Look at what Jesus said in John 14:23–24:

> *Anyone who loves me will obey my teaching. My Father will love them, and we will come to them and make our home with them. Anyone who does not love me will not obey my teaching. These words you hear are not my own; they belong to the Father who sent me.*
>
> **—John 14:23–24** (NIV)

Just as Christ forgave you, you must forgive others.

It's not a suggestion; it's a command. If I'm struggling with forgiving, that's one thing, but struggling with it is not an excuse not to overcome it. Proverbs 3:5 says, "Trust in the LORD with all thine heart" (KJV). Trust that God can help you to do this, because it is possible in some circumstances that you cannot forgive another person on your own. You need God to aid you, because we as humans keep records of wrong (1 Corinthians 13:5). God will separate our sins from us as far as the east is from the west (Psalm 103:12).

That's how God does it. If I try to practice forgiveness on my own, I may fail, but when God comes in, He can make me do things that I can never do alone.

Forgiveness and Love

Galatians 5:1 instructs: "Stand fast therefore in the liberty by which Christ has made us free, and do not be entangled again with a yoke of bondage" (NKJV).

Everything that God asks you to do in the Bible is impossible. He says to love your enemies, to pray for those who violate you. You want to get revenge. You want them to pay, but God is asking you to forgive. Everything that God is asking you to do requires God's help for you to do it. God wants you to depend on Him as He does these things through you.

So, you are free in Christ, but there is a possibility of you being entangled again. Not everybody who is saved is free, because there are certain things that can take you back to the way you used to behave. Your flesh is used to what you used to do when you were in sin. My mom used to say that criticizing your neighbor's garden doesn't pull out the weeds in your own (Matthew 7:1–5).

So, what is forgiveness? It is acknowledging the hurt and confronting it. Don't minimize the pain, but in your own pain show mercy by letting go of the wrong. That means releasing the pain tied to the wrong so that it no longer has power over you.

Have you ever invited people to your house, and while you are eating there is a discussion at the table, and suddenly somebody gets fired up? That discussion took the person back to a place where he or she was hurt before, a place he or she has never moved away from. You can never conquer what you don't confront.[4] You must face it and then live free from bitterness. It is an attitude change.

Forgiveness only takes one person. Reconciliation takes two. You cannot restore a relationship alone, but you can do your part and forgive.

For forgiveness to become your lifestyle, it must first become a habit. When it has been a habit long enough, it eventually becomes a lifestyle. You may wonder what I mean by a "lifestyle of forgiveness." It means you can forgive everyone for everything every time. You don't forgive someone because that person deserves it. You forgive because you want to go higher, and you cannot fly with the weight of another person holding you down.

What Forgiveness Is Not

Oftentimes, our misconceptions of forgiveness can hold us back from truly forgiving someone. Here is a list to help clarify what forgiveness does not entail:

Forgiveness is not approval. Some of us don't forgive people because we feel that if we forgive them, we have condoned the action. That isn't the case. Don't be afraid of forgiving people because you are scared of approving what they did.

Forgiveness is not forgetting or pretending that something never happened. It means changing your original intention. When the person first hurt you, you wanted to hurt the person back, but when you forgive, although you will still remember what he or she did, you give up your right to hit back. You decide not to hurt the other person.

Forgiveness is not justifying. Unfortunately, people often justify their actions through facts. You know I'm sick; that's a fact, but it doesn't justify you being mean. You were drunk—another fact—but that does not justify the fact that you punched me. Some of you adults reading this have marriages that are not doing well because you have hurt each other at one point. Okay, so, that's a fact, but it doesn't justify you having a dead marriage. Don't let one act define a lifetime. Don't allow one season to define the entire year, because there are seasons when there are no leaves on the tree, but when spring comes, everything changes. You need to understand that you cannot define your entire lifetime through one act.

Forgiveness is not an obligation—it's a choice. You cannot force anyone to forgive you.

Forgiveness is not giving in. You have the right to refuse further pain, hurt, and abuse. When I forgive you, I have a right to say, "Please don't call me again. Delete my number from your phone, and don't expect any more calls from me."

Forgiveness is not reconciliation. Forgiveness is not restoration. My forgiveness of you doesn't mean that we are restored. It doesn't mean we will ever go back and hang out together. Forgiveness is not that. Forgiveness is what comes before reconciliation. In other words, you cannot reconcile before you forgive. And forgiving must be complete.

Why is it important to clarify what forgiveness is and what it is not? Because many people mistake forgiveness for restoration, and so they are caught in a self-destructive cycle they keep repeating. They let the offender back into their lives, thinking forgiveness requires them to do so. Forgiveness is releasing the need for repayment, not restoring the relationship.

Sometimes forgiveness means staying in place and working through things, but other times it means you need to leave where you are and start fresh somewhere else. Let me show you what I mean.

On occasion, elders in the church make mistakes and fall. They receive forgiveness from the church, but when they come to me and say they want to be elders again, I tell them no. See, this congregation doesn't change that quickly. They remember. I tell the former elder to look for another place to start fresh.

Forgiveness and trust are not the same thing. When I forgive you, it doesn't mean I trust you again. In other words, when you forgive somebody, you are releasing that person and releasing yourself so that when you are in the same room, nobody has to have a hard time. You can look at each other and smile and you keep moving forward.

Some people forgive and immediately put their trust in the other person again. They will give the offender keys to their apartment or share secrets. Then they get upset when the other person takes their possessions (again) or gossips about them (again).

It doesn't mean that you haven't forgiven somebody if you don't trust them. I have been asked before if you have really forgiven someone if you remember what happened. Well, since forgiveness is not forgetting, then remembering doesn't mean you have an unforgiving heart. It is possible that you will always remember what happened to you.

Also, because forgiveness is not approval, *standing your ground is not unforgiveness*. But the devil whispers, "You would back down if you were a real Christian." Forgiveness is important. Moving forward is important, but remember what I just said. Forgiveness is not trust. Let God work through you, but don't let the devil preach sermons that are not in the Bible.

People hurt you. They left a scar. Forgiveness means that once in a while, when you look at the scar, instead of being reminded of the hurt, you will celebrate the healing. You're looking at the same scar. It hasn't changed, and the one who caused it hasn't changed, but when you have forgiven, you can look at the scar and look at God, and you can celebrate God's deliverance.

Here's my question to you right now: Who are you so mad at that you are willing to spoil how your life turns out? Who is worth sacrificing your divine purpose for?

Who is keeping you up late at night? Do you realize you are making a person who has wronged you powerful? God says, "Be angry, and do not sin: do not let the sun go down on your wrath" (Ephesians 4:26 NKJV).

Let me say this another way. You don't have to sin because you're angry at someone. God is essentially saying, "Put a limit to your heart." That means you shouldn't give the anger more than twenty-four hours. Don't lose sleep over it. Don't lose your appetite. Let it go. It's over.

That's how much God wants you to be free. Think about smelling a trash can. That's exactly what you're breathing in when you don't forgive. You have a time limit on keeping your trash. You get it out of the house every day. You have someone collect all of it once a week. You don't want your trash piling up. But when you don't forgive, that is what your spiritual life is like.

Now, let me talk to the parents reading this. What you do in your family affects how your kids will relate to God. There are some people in the church today who were raised by very tough parents. These people will say that they demand certain standards be maintained in church, but what they really mean is that they want certain practices and behaviors to stay in place. We become what our parents were unless the blood of Christ sets us free. Unless you are delivered, you will become the person—good or bad—who raised you.

None of us came from perfect families. All of us come from a background we didn't choose, but that's why reading the Word of God becomes real; that's why Jesus in your life becomes real; that's why you need prayer so much. It is because there's some bad stuff in you that can flourish without the confrontation of heaven.

Look at Ephesians 4:25–26 and you will see that forgiveness is a process.

Therefore, putting away lying, "Let each one of you speak truth with his neighbor," for we are members of one another. "Be angry, and do not sin": do not let the sun go down on your wrath...
>   —***Ephesians 4:25–26*** (NKJV)

Forgiveness isn't an event; it is a process, but if you choose not to forgive someone or something, then that person or circumstance will remain a lifetime prisoner inside of you. There is life after the argument and the hurt. Don't hold someone hostage because you are not willing to move on. Ephesians 4:25–26 lays out a process to follow:

- Put away lying.

- Speak the truth.

- Remember we are members of one another.

- Be angry.

- But do not sin.

- Do not let the sun go down on your wrath.

So, in other words, you're going to put a limit on the time between when someone wrongs you and when you choose to forgive. There are practical steps to forgiveness, and sometimes there may even be only one simple step required: letting go of a hurt. Other times, it goes deeper, and you need help. I want to bring this to a practical level for you. Forgiveness is about getting to a place where the pain of what happened is gone and the focus is on how

God turned it to good. This is critical, because we are held accountable for what we did do and for what we did not do. Whether we sin against God by commission or omission, there are consequences that will result from our sin. God wants us to be able to live free of those consequences, which is why He promises to help us in this process.

WORKBOOK

Chapter Two Questions

Question: *You know you have authentically forgiven when you no longer define the offender by the offense.* How does Christ model this? Who in your life have you identified by their offense?

_____

_____

_____

_____

_____

_____

_____

_____

_____

_____

_____

Question: What does it mean that you and your offenders have a common enemy? Can you see the spiritual brokenness that led to their offense against you?

_____

_____

_____

_____

_____

_____

_____

_____

_____

_____

_____

Question: Why is it important to differentiate between forgiveness and trust?

_____

_____

_____

_____

_____

_____

_____

_____

_____

_____

_____

_____

Action: On a blank piece of paper, draw a line down the middle. On one side, write "Forgiveness Is," and on the other side, write "Forgiveness Is Not." Fill in each column with a bulleted list of what you have learned already in this book. Then continue to add items as you read the following chapters.

Chapter Two Notes

CHAPTER THREE

God's Forgiveness

And forgive us our debts, as we also have forgiven our debtors.

—Matthew 6:12 *(NIV)*

We often quote the Lord's Prayer, but do you take the time to really look at what Jesus said, especially as it pertains to the idea of forgiveness? In the Lord's Prayer, we ask God to forgive us in the same way that we forgive others. You cannot hold other people hostage in your heart through unforgiveness and expect God to freely forgive you. It's amazing that all of us ask for grace for ourselves, and we ask for justice for everybody else. Think about how many times you've prayed that prayer and asked God to offer the same level of grace to you that you've offered to other people.

That means that if you are not forgiving other people, you are also living under condemnation. If your life stinks, this could be why. Grace is not flowing through you, so your spirit becomes like a stagnant pond. Nothing alive exists in stagnant water. You cannot get fresh water from a pond where nothing is happening. Even if water flows in continually, if there isn't a channel for water to continue, all you see is death. The Dead Sea receives water, but then the water evaporates away, leaving salt and minerals that cannot support life.

In the same way, your life becomes dead when you only receive grace from others and do not extend it to people who have hurt you. If you are praying the Lord's Prayer and asking Him to forgive you the way that you forgive other people, then you are setting up conditions. It means that God will only do for us what we do for others. That is seriously important to anybody who needs forgiveness from God. You are saying, "God, forgive me. Help me, Jesus," and Jesus is saying, "Yes, I want to, but who are *you* forgiving?"

You have certainly heard that people who hurt others have been hurt themselves.[5] That is little consolation when you have suffered a wrong. You don't want to make excuses for another person's bad behavior—particularly your own—but understanding why a person does something can sometimes make it easier for you to get to a place where you can forgive the person. Try to put yourself in his or her shoes and see what happened through his or her experience, in his or her perceptions or misperceptions, and with his or her impressions. Even if you don't fully agree, after you forgive, you may then know how to avoid another misunderstanding.

So, let me give you some reasons why you should forgive those who hurt you:

Anyone that you haven't forgiven controls you, because the individual is also controlling your emotions. You want to forgive the person because you want control. I will always know who you have an issue with by how you react when the person walks into the room. You want to be submitted to no one except God.

You want peace. If you aren't willing to forgive, then you won't have peace. In order to move on, you have to let what happened go. Forgiveness does not remove the incident from your memory, but it does cut the chains that bind you to that memory.

The Bible tells us to put away wrath, anger, clamor, and evil speaking, with all malice (Ephesians 4:31 KJV). Bitterness is something that should never exist in our hearts. When you are bitter, it affects everything around you, and when you don't forgive, negative things have a way of giving birth to other negative things. Every sin has a family. When you don't forgive, you feel bad and sometimes hatred comes in. When hatred is so pregnant that it must give birth to something, bitterness comes in.

And when bitterness becomes full, you can become someone you don't recognize. You will wonder how your anger got so strong. It is because you allowed one thing to mature. That is why forgiving must become first a habit and then a lifestyle. You must forgive everyone for everything every time. I may be mad at you, but when I go to sleep, I want to be thanking God for you. You may not be able to reconcile with everyone, but you can forgive, because forgiveness only needs one person; reconciliation needs two.

You want to be complete emotionally, physically, and spiritually, and you can only have that completion in you when you forgive. Some of us run to church to hide away from life. I have discovered that God is not looking for a crazy few who just live in the church. He wants people who are effective in the community because they are healed completely. You cannot serve God when you're holding on to someone else. Even worse than this, by not forgiving, you are allowing Satan to do his work through you. You are allowing disobedience to stop God's work through you on the earth.

Unforgiveness produces loveless lives. For example, you might have a church where a bunch of people are fighting and won't forgive each other, but they sing songs about surrender and victory. If you look at your life and it doesn't have the peace and victory you would like it to have, consider where you are spiritually. If there is anger and fighting in your house, then you need to deal with it through prayer and action. You cannot argue and fight with your spouse all the time and expect peace in your home. You are modeling that behavior to your kids. Worse still is when a parent talks down about the other parent to their child or about one child to another. The Bible says that love covers a multitude of sins (1 Peter 4:8 ESV). Doesn't that sound like forgiveness to you? So, holding a grudge against someone isn't love. You must forgive because you want to love. You cannot love before you forgive; it doesn't work.

> Two people owed money to a certain moneylender. One owed him five hundred denarii, and the other fifty. Neither of them had the money to pay him back, so he forgave the debts of both. Now which of them will love him more? Simon replied, "I suppose the one who had the bigger debt forgiven." "You have judged correctly," Jesus said.
> —**Luke 7:41–43** (NIV)

There is an important lesson in this passage. People will sometimes try to look like they are spiritual giants, but you cannot be a spiritual giant without having been forgiven of much. The text says that it was the one who was forgiven of much who loves much (Luke 7:47 NKJV).

Love and respect are two sides of the same emotion. You see, men need respect in the way that women need love.[6] If a woman doesn't show respect to her husband or speaks in a way that makes him feel she doesn't respect him, it hurts him as deeply and in the same way as when a man speaks to his wife in an unloving manner.

Why are love and respect important to forgiveness? Because both are about the way a person feels. It's a matter of the time you give a person—both the quantity of time and the quality of time. Quality is the product of quantity. When you put in more time with a person, you get to know him or her better, and you learn how to show him or her love and respect. The same is true in our time with God.

As you spend that time in God's presence, you become more like Him and you want to do things that please Him. You want to improve that relationship. When you were saved, it was like the start of a marriage. The wedding is just the beginning. The same is true with God; salvation is just the beginning. The relationship develops as we grow to be more like God, and as we show Him respect by doing what He asks. As we show Him love by wanting to be more like Him, we grow a deeper relationship with Him. And as our relationship with Him deepens, our love for other people deepens, because His love flows through us.

When we are not mature in the Lord, our behavior doesn't always line up perfectly, and God understands this. However, we should continue to deepen the relationship. You must get down to the root of your behavior and not focus on the branches (the fruit). In other words, you cannot forgive people (fruit) without becoming more like God on the inside (root).

Ephesians 4:32 has this to say: "And be kind to one another, tenderhearted, forgiving one another, even as God in Christ forgave you" (NKJV).

God is Abba, Daddy, and He wants us to want to be like Him. In order to be more like Him, we must forgive as He forgave. You are like God when you forgive, because if you take the forgiveness of God out of the Bible, there is no Bible. The Bible is a book of forgiveness, and God is calling us to have our own book of forgiveness, too. The standard of forgiveness is forgiving because God forgives.

Moreover, the Bible says to be kind to one another. That means people who forgive are kind people. Some of us don't even know what kindness means because we're mean all the time. Forgiveness is not what you say; it's how you make the other person feel. Be kind to one another, tender-hearted, forgiving one another.

Pay particular attention to your families, because what happens in the family hurts deeper than anything else, because in the family—as in the church—relationships are built on trust.

This is particularly important for men, because the Bible warns husbands that the way they treat their wives can impact their prayers. Peter says, "Likewise, husbands, live with your wives in an understanding way, showing honor to the woman as the weaker vessel, since they are heirs with you of the grace of life, so that your prayers may not be hindered" (ESV).

When you come into a relationship with God, you don't live your life for you. Notice what the Bible says.

> Therefore if you bring your gift to the altar, and there remember that your brother has something against you, leave your gift there before the altar, and go your way. First be reconciled to your brother, and then come and offer your gift.
> —**Matthew 5:23–24** (NKJV)

When you're going to church and it comes to your mind that there's a brother who has an issue with you, you are told to go and reconcile. The text doesn't imply that you have an issue with a brother, but that the brother has an issue with you. You may not be angry, but if the Holy

Spirit is telling you that someone is in bondage over you, then you have power to free him or her.

The church only moves forward at the speed of its weakest member, because God calls on us to help him or her. You can see this in Paul's teachings, where he said he doesn't do things—even if they are not sinful—if they offend another person, because he doesn't want to cause offense (1 Corinthians 8:9–13; 1 Corinthians 10:23–33). He also says not to dress in a way that might cause another to stumble, even if the clothes are not sinful.

You can see this same principle in the account of the Israelites in the desert. When the spies went to the Promised Land, they explored, then came back, and ten of them said they were like grasshoppers compared to the people in the land, but Joshua and Caleb said, "Right now we can go and take it" (Numbers 13:30). Despite the faith of these two, the Israelites were forced to walk in the wilderness for a generation. That is because God knew the spiritually mature people would trust Him as they wandered. The others needed to get to a place where they would trust God, so everyone could have the victory.

When I was growing up, I was the only one in my family who attended church, and during that time I was entirely focused on church. That's not a bad thing, unless you neglect your schoolwork and your responsibility to your family, like I was doing. I thought I was doing right, but if you're neglecting your obligations just to be at church, you are in sin.

I didn't realize the impact that what I was doing had on me and my family's perception of God. My dad took me in our car to talk to me. He put his foot on the gas and the brake at the same time. The engine screamed, and smoke started to come out of the engine, but we weren't going anywhere.

"Dad," I said, "what are you doing?"

"I want you to understand that sometimes you think you are making progress because of the sound of the engine, but when your foot is on the brake, you are staying in the same place," he answered.

That is a strong bit of wisdom. At that time, I was so involved in church that I was doing poorly in school. My dad didn't get angry at my church activity, but he demonstrated to me that I couldn't go forward if I was limiting my future. I couldn't become a pastor if I couldn't even finish high school.

I want you to think about it in light of what we're talking about. In fact, we are living that illustration from my dad. We have the gas and the brakes on at the same time. You feel like you can do something great, but something always holds you back. You are attending church and you are on committees, but God cannot use you because you haven't forgiven a choir director who offended you when you were a new Christian thirty years ago.

Do you know how many times I visit people who are still mad because when they got pregnant forty-five years ago, they were kicked out of church because they weren't married? I was not the pastor when it happened, but they are still angry at our church. People are angry at the body of Christ and refuse to attend church because a Christian hurt them, but we are doing no better, because as believers we won't forgive someone for saying something hurtful.

It is going to affect your relationship with God if you don't let it go. Think about it. John says if we say that we have no sin, we deceive ourselves and the truth is not in us. That means all of us have wronged somebody. All of us.

Now, think again about the Israelites. They couldn't move forward until everyone was ready to enter the Promised Land. Could it be that your church, or even your family, isn't able to move forward into God's plan for their lives because there is someone at church whom you hurt—whether you knew it or not—and the person is waiting to hear you say, "I'm sorry"? All the person wants is to be heard. Have you taken the time to ask God if there is anyone whom you've offended or whom you're angry at and need to forgive? Are you willing to do that?

> *If we say that we have no sin, we deceive ourselves, and the truth is not in us. If we confess our sins, He is faithful and just to forgive us our sins and to cleanse us from all unrighteousness. If we say that we have not sinned, we make Him a liar, and His word is not in us.*
> *—1 John 1:8–10 (NKJV)*

You can gather from these verses that holding unforgiveness in your heart toward someone costs you more than it costs that individual.

So, now, how do you fix this? If you confess your sins, He is faithful and just to forgive your sins and cleanse you from all unrighteousness. Then you become more like God by forgiving more like God. You need to make God the reason you do everything. God wants you to get to the point of saying that you love and forgive the other person because of Him. Get beyond the benefit to yourself; do it because of God.

I've learned that with forgiveness, sometimes you need to learn to let everything go and see what remains. There is so much clutter in our lives because we don't know what to let go of. The fastest way to know what you need to let go of is to let everything go and see what remains.

Forgiveness benefits you, it frees the other person, and it improves your relationship with God. And when I forgive you, it doesn't mean I condone what you did, but I want my relationship with God to get better. This is an important part of spiritual maturity and drawing others to the Kingdom. If you want your behavior to be an example of how you want God to relate to you, then stop worrying about what someone else might get away with and, instead, look at what you're missing out on in God's kingdom. God never calls you to do something that He isn't able to do through you. Become a willing vessel.

WORKBOOK

Chapter Three Questions

Question: How should God's forgiveness of you inform and motivate your forgiveness of others?

_____

_____

_____

_____

_____

_____

_____

_____

_____

_____

Question: How does unforgiveness hinder your usability for God or hold you back from fulfilling His call?

_____

_____

_____

_____

_____

_____

_____

_____

_____

_____

_____

Question: What is your responsibility before God if you know that someone maintains unforgiveness toward you?

_____

_____

_____

_____

_____

_____

_____

_____

_____

_____

_____

Action: In your journal, write "God has forgiven me…" and record examples of how God has forgiven, reconciled, and restored you, personally. Spend time thanking and praising Him for His lavish forgiveness.

_____

_____

_____

_____

_____

_____

_____

_____

_____

_____

_____

_____

_____

_____

Chapter Three Notes

_____

_____

_____

_____

_____

_____

_____

_____

_____

_____

_____

_____

_____

_____

_____

_____

_____

_____

_____

_____

CHAPTER FOUR

Forgiving Yourself

In this chapter, we are going to start to deal with some difficult questions of forgiveness. It feels nice to say that we need to forgive and to think about the benefits of forgiving others, but what about forgiveness when the pain is still very real?

Look at Romans 7:15–20. This passage was written by the apostle Paul, a man who was so close to God that even handkerchiefs and aprons that had touched him healed people (Acts 19:11–12). In these verses, Paul is talking about the sin that dwells in him. Sometimes we praise God so much that we forget that sin dwells in us. All you need is someone to cut you off in traffic, and suddenly you hear the sin coming from your mouth. We are wired to sin, which is why I thank God when I get caught for the little stuff, because I don't want to know what big sins still lurk in me.

I do not understand what I do. For what I want to do I do not do, but what I hate I do. And if I do what I do not want

*to do, I agree that the law is good. As it is, it is no longer I
myself who do it, but it is sin living in me. For I know that
good itself does not dwell in me, that is, in my sinful nature.
For I have the desire to do what is good, but I cannot carry
it out. For I do not do the good I want to do, but the evil I
do not want to do—this I keep on doing. Now if I do what
I do not want to do, it is no longer I who do it, but it is sin
living in me that does it.*

—Romans 7:15–20 *(NIV)*

Think about your own life. When you make a mistake—when you sin—it isn't because you don't know the right thing to do, but rather, it is because you don't do the right thing. Paul is saying here that he is a victim of the sin that lives inside of him. It is the same for you. It is the same with other people. Sometimes we know what we need to do, but our lower nature wins out and we find ourselves making the wrong choice.

Everybody has got something that he or she never wants anybody to know about. There is a deep sin that you are so ashamed of that you may even live fearing that someday that sin will be exposed. God's grace covers it. God is the only One who will never expose you to other people, yet you may still live with the guilt and you may worry that one day God will punish you for your secret sin. However, God promises that when we confess our sin and accept Jesus' sacrifice, our sin is paid for (1 John 1:9). The problem is that while God forgives, others still remind us of the guilt. This makes it difficult for us to really believe that the sin is gone and paid for.

Guilt is incredibly strong, and it can remain dormant inside us and come back in times of weakness or loss. In 1 Kings 17, we see a mighty prophet of God named Elijah.

He was fed by the ravens at the brook during a famine (1 Kings 17:2–7). After a time there, while God provided for Elijah, eventually the brook dried up, and God told him to go to Zarephath to find a widow (1 Kings 17:8–16). This woman was ready to prepare her last meal before dying with her son, due to the famine in the land. Elijah went to her and said:

> Do not fear; go and do as you have said, but make me a small cake from it first, and bring it to me; and afterward make some for yourself and your son. For thus says the LORD God of Israel: "The bin of flour shall not be used up, nor shall the jar of oil run dry, until the day the Lord sends rain on the earth."
>
> **—1 Kings 17:13–14** (NKJV)

She obeyed, and because she did, she survived. This is an example of a breakthrough. In our own lives, if we live through something difficult and then have a great breakthrough, we feel relieved and empowered. Even if it is only daily provision, we see it as mighty power every day. Certainly, this is how these three felt at that time. While the famine raged around them, they were sitting in God's daily provision and seeing their needs met.

One day, though, this all changed, and just like we typically do, the woman sought out an explanation for the setback. This is how the Bible records it:

> Sometime later, the son of the woman who owned the house became ill. He grew worse and worse, and finally stopped breathing. She said to Elijah, "What do you have

against me, man of God? Did you come to remind me of my
sin and kill my son?"

—1 Kings 17:17–18 *(NIV)*

It is possible to live in a miracle, like this woman did, and still have guilt from something that happened a long time ago. The Bible never tells us what her sin was, but that makes the story even more universal in its application. When something bad happens to another person, we immediately search for an explanation. We try to find some weakness in the person's faith, or a hidden sin that would have caused the setback. We do the same in our own lives, but usually the process ends with our defense. We say things like, "I gave my tithe. I attend church three times a week. I led two people to the Lord last month. Why is this happening to me?"

Look again at this woman's story and see what you can learn about forgiveness and guilt. From her question, it seems that she thought the blessing of food came because God had forgotten her sin. Therefore, when something went wrong, she then concluded that He had suddenly remembered her sin. It is amazing how tragedy and trouble can make people behave. Truthfully, many of us actually believe that God is out to get us.

Some people aren't running to Jesus, but rather, they are running from their past. You will never enjoy God if what you are focused on is what you are escaping. Bad things aren't happening to you because God is trying to teach you a lesson. He won't give you cancer, shut down your kidneys, or destroy your marriage to help you rely more on Him.

What would you learn through those experiences? That it hurt? Simply because God permits things does not mean He causes things. This belief causes some people to run to church because of their guilt and their fear of the past. It also leads many people to run away from God out of bitterness and hurt. We have to recognize that we live in a world filled with disappointments, sickness, and diseases. We should run to the arms of God in these difficult times, but when we think He is the one who sent the difficulties, why would we ever run to Him?

That leads me to my next point. You must learn to give yourself forgiveness as you learn. This world teaches us to accuse ourselves. Sometimes you are your own worst enemy. You hate your height, or your weight, or your skin color, or even your parents.

You need to recognize your own need for forgiveness. Help never comes until you admit that you have a problem. You cannot get to where you need to go without knowing where you are. For so many of us, our growth and freedom are being postponed because we are denying where we actually are.

You are not happy, but you try to look that way by filling your life with things. Instead, you need to start by saying, "Look, I'm a problem because I'm a sinner. Sin dwells in me; there are some things that I do, some words that I say, some bad feelings that I cause, and because of that, I am a problem."

Once you realize that you're a problem, you also know you need forgiveness. If you don't admit that you do wrong, you cannot forgive yourself. Often, when someone has hurt us, there is some culpability on both sides. Take time to see what role you have played yourself when a relationship has been damaged or someone has been hurt.

Not everything negative people say about us is a lie. When we hear something, especially from someone close to us or who knows us well, we need to take a close look at ourselves to see if there is truth and then deal with it. I may not like what the person says, but I need to admit when there is an issue and then communicate with God to get rid of the sin that is uncovered.

Many of us are masters at deceiving ourselves. We act like we have everything together, but we are full of sin in our lives. The Bible says that, if we say we have no sin, we deceive ourselves (1 John 1:8 NKJV). We need to admit our part. That doesn't justify the offender, but it releases us.

In order for you to forgive yourself, you must name the offenders and the offenses. This is because when our feelings are involved, we can sometimes bring up lots of other things that are already under the blood. Isolate the issue. After you are confronted, you have to let the issue die in your mind.

This widow hadn't done that. She didn't have the blood of Jesus to aid her, but the prophet of God had been brought to her home to provide for her. Certainly, if God had wanted to meet her physical needs for food, He also wanted to meet her emotional and spiritual needs. This is our God. He found this woman out of all the people who were experiencing the famine, and He sent His prophet to her to bring healing. Unfortunately, she was so aware of her sin that it held on to her. Are you suffering from the same thing? How long had the prophet been in her home, but she was still holding on to this sin memory? Then, when it looked like something was going wrong again, she immediately pulled up the sin as an explanation for her suffering.

Everything around you has an expiration date stamped on it somewhere. You need to put the expiration stamp on your anger and not carry it around. Don't waste your life by being angry. Allow yourself to move on. Get an accountability partner who will say something when you try to pick up the guilt again or when you start to feel resentment against someone you've already forgiven—but then move on. Keep moving forward.

In Ephesians 4:25–26, the apostle Paul tells us that there is a time limit: "Therefore, putting away lying, 'Let each one of you speak truth with his neighbor,' for we are members of one another. 'Be angry, and do not sin': do not let the sun go down on your wrath" (NKJV).

Leave the Past Behind

The only way to change your past is to forgive it. Philippians 3:13 states, "Brethren, I do not count myself to have apprehended; but one thing I do, forgetting those things which are behind and reaching forward to those things which are ahead..." (NKJV).

Everyone has a past. You cannot reach forward while you are reaching back. The only way to change your past is to forgive it. The past is the past and there is nothing you can do to fix what has already been done. If you want to hurt yourself, just think about those things that you cannot change.

Instead make your future greater than your past, because if God is going to do anything amazing in your life, it is going to be in your future. Don't underestimate what your future can bring, and don't overestimate what your past took away from you.

If your past were all that you were supposed to have, then you would have died in your past. The fact that you have survived your past means that your past didn't kill you. Your happiness was not left back there; there is going to be something in the now. But you have been looking backward for so long that you are missing opportunities on which you are standing.

There is a story in a book called *Acres of Diamonds*[7] about the largest diamond mine in South Africa, called the Kimberly Diamond Mine. The story is told that there was a guy who owned the farm, and there was a little river that ran through his farm. The man who owned this farm went everywhere on the continent trying to collect minerals. On one of these adventures while searching for new minerals, he left but never returned to his own farm.

Years later, someone was passing through this farm and looked down in the stream, kicking the rocks and looking for minerals just as the previous owner had done before. The person found a shiny stone. That shiny stone turned out to be a diamond. The stream was full of them. That small farm became the largest diamond mine in the world. The Kimberly Diamond Mine was literally in his backyard, but he had been looking too far for what he was standing directly on top of.

There are many of us who are standing on diamonds right now, but because we think our deliverance is going to cost us too much, we are missing out on opportunities that God has in our life right here, right now. Jesus says, "So if the Son sets you free, you will be free indeed" (John 8:36 NIV), and He says that "you will know the truth, and the truth will set you free" (John 8:32 NIV). After you have forgiven yourself, true freedom comes from Jesus— knowing Him, embracing Him, allowing Him to live in you.

Where the Spirit of God is, there is liberty and freedom. Freedom doesn't come from lying to yourself. It doesn't come from covering up for yourself. You have to face yourself. Once you have done so, recognize that God knows you even better than you know yourself, and He wants to use you in His kingdom. Accept His gift of forgiveness. Forgive yourself. That is how you will make a great future. Don't wander off searching for this thing that will make you happy. True happiness comes with forgiveness in Christ and with forgiving yourself.

Chapter Four Questions

Question: What brought the widow's sense of guilt to the surface? Describe a time when you thought a bad thing that happened to you was God punishing you for past sin.

_____

_____

_____

_____

_____

_____

_____

_____

_____

_____

_____

Question: What is the difference between God permitting things and God causing things? When difficulties come, do you tend to run to God or away from Him?

_____

_____

_____

_____

_____

_____

_____

_____

_____

_____

_____

Question: What are things for which you need to forgive yourself? In what particular areas do you need to leave the past behind?

_____

_____

_____

_____

_____

_____

_____

_____

_____

_____

_____

_____

Action: Plan a time to talk with a counselor, pastor, or accountability partner about areas in which you have trouble forgiving yourself.

Chapter Four Notes

CHAPTER FIVE

When God Disappoints You

We don't like to talk about when we feel disappointed by something that God has done—or has not done—in our life or in a situation we are facing. In fact, we may feel it is somehow wrong to even feel the emotion without articulating it. However, there are times when we do feel that way, and God already knows we do. Hiding this feeling doesn't make it go away; instead, as we discussed in the previous chapter, holding on to the feeling of hurt just hurts us.

We will see in the Bible that others have felt this way, too, but God has teachings in His Word to help us when we do have these feelings. God wants our love and respect, but He also knows that we have a limited understanding. While feeling angry at God doesn't help us, it is something that He understands and wants to help us with.

So, what do you do when you need deliverance from the One with whom you are angry? You may be preaching or teaching in the church or singing in the choir, but that doesn't mean you are right with God. It is like holding a grudge against your spouse. If you are angry, there will be strife in the home. If you feel offended by God, your mindset will be messed up, and it will limit His ability to help you.

Let's look at two foundational Bible passages.

> *Now it came to pass, when Jesus finished commanding His twelve disciples, that He departed from there to teach and to preach in their cities.*
>
> *And when John had heard in prison about the works of Christ, he sent two of his disciples and said to Him, "Are You the Coming One, or do we look for another?"*
>
> *Jesus answered and said to them, "Go and tell John the things which you hear and see: The blind see and the lame walk; the lepers are cleansed and the deaf hear; the dead are raised up and the poor have the gospel preached to them. And blessed is he who is not offended because of Me."*
> *—Matthew 11:1–6 (NKJV)*

The John referred to here is John the Baptist. He was in prison for preaching against Herod and he was feeling frustrated. John knew he had been living out his purpose, but now he was in prison and he wondered if he had been right or not. Where was the great redemption that he thought was coming? Jesus' answer seems to indicate that John was angry or bitter, because He talked about offense. Maybe John needed encouragement or maybe he was upset because he was questioning everything he had believed and taught. Either way, John's hurt was clear, and Jesus addressed it in a rather unusual way. Let's look at another prophet's writing, and then I'll show you what you can learn from both of these men.

> When God saw what they did and how they turned from their evil ways, he relented and did not bring on them the destruction he had threatened.
>
> But to Jonah this seemed very wrong, and he became angry. He prayed to the LORD, "Isn't this what I said, LORD, when I was still at home? That is what I tried to forestall by fleeing to Tarshish. I knew that you are a gracious and compassionate God, slow to anger and abounding in love, a God who relents from sending calamity. Now, LORD, take away my life, for it is better for me to die than to live."
> —*Jonah 3:10–4:3 (NIV)*

God had sent Jonah to decree destruction on the Ninevites, but when they repented, God changed His mind and didn't destroy them. This made Jonah angry. You would think the preacher would have shouted for joy from the rooftops for the redemption of the city, but he was upset by it.

The Bible next says that Jonah prayed, which means that he still had a prayer life. Some of us get mad because something is unclear and so we don't pray. God can handle our attitude. He wants us to be honest with Him, because He already knows what we are feeling. When we talk to Him, we are being honest with ourselves and then we start on the path to healing.

Jonah was frustrated because he knew of God's mercy and that God would forgive the Ninevites if they repented. Jonah said that he wanted to die rather than see the mercy come to his enemy. He even tried to kill himself by jumping off the boat, but God rescued him. Now he was asking God to kill him.

Jonah and John had a dilemma. They were different, but both accounts contain similar lessons that we can learn from.

Jonah entered the city stinking like fish and preaching with an attitude. His sermon was short and to the point. As we learn at the end of his story, he really didn't want to see the deliverance of the city, but rather he wanted to boast of their coming destruction. The Bible says that the people repented.

Here is what I want you to see: simply because you are successful spiritually doesn't mean that your mind or heart is right. Don't be easily impressed by people simply because God chooses to bless others through them. While it is true that the Bible says that we can see fruit and we are to judge it (Matthew 7:15–20), it is also true that God gave examples of using the ungodly to accomplish His purposes on earth (Habakkuk 1:5–11). Fruit is more than just results. Fruit is the life that the person leads and the condition of someone's heart.

Jonah doesn't say he is mad at God because of what God has done, but rather because of who God is. Maybe Jonah believed that if he didn't go to the city, then the condemnation would come on the Ninevites because they couldn't repent. Maybe he felt he was sacrificing his life as a martyr by jumping off of the ship and destroying the enemy of his people? One thing is very clear: Jonah didn't want God's mercy to be extended to these people.

There are only two books in the Bible that end with a question. Jonah is one of them. It's a book that ends with a question from God that Jonah never answers (Jonah 4:10–11).

Jonah showed in this book that he didn't have a forgiving heart toward the Ninevites and all those who would be impacted. Furthermore, he didn't have God's heart of love, compassion, and mercy. While he was a prophet, his story isn't recorded as an example of obedience. However, while Jonah initially tried to avoid God's call, we can see that he finally did what God told him to do, even when he didn't like it or understand it. He was real with God.

John the Baptist also struggled with understanding what God was doing. He heard that his cousin, Jesus, was doing great things while John was in prison. John had seen the divine protection Jesus had lived through and had no doubt been told of God's protection of Jesus from His birth forward. Maybe he'd heard stories from his mother about how his cousin, along with Mary and Joseph, had escaped death by going to Egypt, and how God had provided for the holy family there. John may have been feeling confused and alone, and he was seeking courage and encouragement. He needed to know whether Jesus really was the one he thought He was. Instead of answering directly, Jesus told of what was happening. He didn't simply say yes, but He sent a beautiful picture of what was happening for John to hold on to.

While Jonah and John the Baptist are very different, they can represent two sides of what you experience when you simply don't understand why something is happening. You may feel frustrated at God, because you see someone who has done horrible things get forgiven, but then you also see someone—maybe even you—who tried to do the right thing, only to find his or her ministry limited or stopped just as it was bearing fruit.

When It Feels Unfair

Then the LORD said to Satan, "Have you considered my servant Job? There is no one on earth like him; he is blameless and upright, a man who fears God and shuns evil."

"Does Job fear God for nothing?" Satan replied. "Have you not put a hedge around him and his household and everything he has? You have blessed the work of his hands, so that his flocks and herds are spread throughout the land. But now stretch out your hand and strike everything he has, and he will surely curse you to your face."

The LORD said to Satan, "Very well, then, everything he has is in your power, but on the man himself do not lay a finger."

—Job 1:8–12 (NIV)

Job was a man who probably felt like life was unfair. Not only had he tried to do what was right, but he had tried to teach his children to do the same, and when he was in a time of need, all of his friends abandoned him or spent their time trying to tell him why God was punishing him.

For an entire chapter, Job made his case by laying out all that he'd done to be faithful to God and then complained that God had allowed these bad things to fall upon him (Job 29). He wanted God to come down and explain.

You haven't started serving God until He puts you in a position to be mad at Him. God says that His people perish because of lack of knowledge (Hosea 4:6)—not because of lack of faith, not because they don't keep the Sabbath, not because they're not vegetarians, and not for any other reason. People perish because of lack of knowledge.

Those of us who have served God for even a little while have discovered that God has a way of changing situations. You cannot threaten people and have God as a backup.

That is what happened with Jonah. Jonah did his part, and now he was waiting for the city of Nineveh to be burned. He expected that he'd be the only one alive at the end.

In fact, Jonah 4 says that Jonah was so angry he went to higher ground in order to actually watch the city burn (Jonah 4:1–5). The reality is that not everybody who is saving you wants you saved. Not everybody talking in the church about what you need to do really wants you to do it. Jonah had resisted the call to help these people, and after he did help, even seeing their repentance, he still wanted to see them suffer.

I am going to share some things that may be hard for you to hear, but stay with me, because you'll see at the end how this will help you in your relationship with God.

Jesus may disappoint, but He never fails anyone.

Moses tried to help God by trying to deliver Israel through his own methods: he killed an Egyptian to protect an Israelite (Exodus 2:11–15), and he was on the run for forty years (Acts 7:30).

Joseph was faithful and refused to sin against God when Potiphar's wife came with temptation, but he spent years in jail for his honor instead of being promoted for his faithfulness (Genesis 37:2, Genesis 41:46).

God can disappoint you.

If all of your prayers are to be answered in your lifetime, then you are not praying big enough. Some of the prayers you are praying today are going to be answered in the generations to come, as in the case of generational blessings and curses (Exodus 20:5). For example, King David showed kindness to Mephibosheth for the sake of Mephibosheth's father, Jonathan (2 Samuel 9).

So, we get disappointed, because we want to see the solution right now, and yet God is saying that a day is like a thousand years to the Him (2 Peter 3:8). Don't give up on God.

Don't spiritualize your disappointment. When you say you have an unspoken request, you may really be saying that you are disappointed by God. "Unspoken" usually means we're embarrassed to share what we are thinking, because we think the people in the room will not understand.

All of us experience disappointments because we are human. We may have done the right things, but we don't see the results we have hoped for. Meanwhile, someone who seems to live the wrong way is receiving the blessing for which we have prayed.

We don't have to be wrong to be disappointed; we don't have to be right to be disappointed. Life is just life.

That is why we need to encourage each other. It doesn't matter how spiritual we are: we need encouragement.

When was the last time you picked up your phone and called your pastor just to tell him what a great job he is doing? Do you encourage and pray for members of your family? Do you tell them how much you value them, and do you make them a priority in your life?

Encourage your children, your spouse, and those you love, or they may seek encouragement elsewhere. Whoever is blessing your life needs your support. It doesn't matter who it is.

Why are we disappointed in life? Why are we disappointed by God?

Despite knowing that God loves us and forgiving others, there are still disappointments in life. We are sometimes disappointed with ourselves, and other times we are frustrated with the people around us. Now I want to get real and give you a list of some reasons we may be disappointed by God.

We are disappointed by God because of circumstances. From our perspective, sometimes God is inconsistent. We try to learn formulas because we see something that worked for someone else. We get excited and we try the formula, but then God changes the formula. So, from our perspective, God seems inconsistent.

Look again at John the Baptist. When John was in prison, he may have been thinking, "Jesus, You are blessing people. I'm in jail. What does that mean? Bless me, too" (Matthew 11:2–3). From his perspective, Jesus was delivering others and all He needed to do was say the word to deliver John, as well. Jesus didn't. So, from John's perspective, it was painful. God appeared inconsistent.

We are disappointed because of confusion between the reliability of God and God's predictability. When we cannot predict God, we conclude that He is not reliable. But God says that His ways are not our ways (Isaiah 55:8). In other words, there are things about Him that we cannot understand, but we still try. When we cannot predict how God will deliver us, then we struggle to believe that He will deliver us at all.

Look again at Jonah. He went ahead to Nineveh and preached, expecting the city to be destroyed after he had finished. God said that the wickedness of the Ninevites had come up before Him (Jonah 1:2 NIV). This whole book isn't about the city of Nineveh. It is about one person—Jonah.

Everybody in the book of Jonah repented—except Jonah. There is repentance in every chapter, but in chapter 4, Jonah was the only one who was mad. Even the guys on the ship who threw everything out to help him repented on the ship. They went where they were going with an empty ship, but with a new faith.

God can use you to bless others even when you are not right. Jonah was not in Nineveh because he wanted to go there. Jonah was in Nineveh because the fish took him there. Although you may act like you came to church because you're holy, many of us found Jesus while we were running from Him. He caught us. He messed up our agenda. He disturbed our careers.

That is why you should never look like you are better than anybody else, because whatever you are doing right now is not because you are great. It is because of God's great grace.

We get disappointed because of our failed expectations. All of us have expectations. Failed expectations are at the heart of disappointments. You can see this in many kinds of relationships.

Most of the fights between married people are due to uncommunicated expectations.

Drama in church usually happens because we didn't articulate our expectations. Most of your expectations are not evil; they are just not communicated. Every living relationship has expectations. If we don't speak those clearly, people will get disappointed and hurt.

We get disappointed when we allow our desires to govern our expectations. Whenever you allow your desires to govern your expectations of God, you're destined to be disappointed. As human beings, we are in the struggle of having thoughts and ways that are contrary to God's ways and thoughts. It's not that our desires are always evil, but when we let them control us, we will be disappointed, because ultimately God's desire will supersede. Also, our desires may want to get us out of a situation when the situation is the process to the purpose.

Forgiving God?

Because disappointment is mainly a problem with perception, forgiving God is about fixing that issue. Whenever you are disappointed by God, it is your perception that is wrong. It's not the facts or the reality of things that disappoint you about God. It's the perception. John the Baptist had heard that Jesus was helping other people, so his perception was that if Jesus was doing good things for others, then He could do them for John, too. That shows a misunderstanding of Jesus' mission and why we're all here. Here are some points to understand and remember when you are disappointed by your circumstances:

You need to understand that Jesus came for you, but He didn't come to please you. He isn't here to answer to you.

Jesus came for you. Remember this in the story of Jonah. Jonah went to preach and then to watch the people burn in their destruction, but God changed His mind because the Ninevites repented (Jonah 4:1–11). Jonah was angry that it was in God's nature to forgive. Jonah planned to watch the city be punished, not redeemed.

However, *Jesus demands that you subject yourself to His agenda.* Jesus is the message, and you are the messenger. Don't flip the order there. Don't have a role reversal in your relationship with God. You are the messenger, and He is the message.

The funny thing about being disappointed is that we always seek an explanation. Have you noticed that? You want God to explain why you were disappointed. *But when we are disappointed by God, He never offers an explanation. He only offers Himself.*

See, that's why God says, "Come now, let's reason together." It's not about winning an argument. It's about embracing the person. Jesus doesn't just teach truth. Jesus is the truth (John 14:6).

Let the truth of Jesus live inside of you. It's not what you memorize; it's who you've got on the inside. Some of you reading this have been struggling because of what you have gone through. You have been mad at God because God is an all-powerful, all-knowing God, but He let you marry that no-good man. We are mad at God because if He is all knowing and all-powerful, why didn't He come to our aid?

I want you to understand that God wants you to be addicted to the big picture. It doesn't matter whether or not you can predict Him. *You can trust Him even when you cannot predict Him.* It's not wrong to be mad at God, but understand that *God has your back.*

Every one of us has been hurt, because things always happen in life. Many of us have tears that we cry when we are all alone. Your bathroom may be your crying room, and when you step out you look like all is well, like you're strong. But inside every strong person, there is a little child who is crying, who is mad, who has more questions than answers, and who is, at the end of the day, mad at God.

WORKBOOK

Chapter Five Questions

Question: Describe a situation in which you felt disappointed or even angry with God. Were you honest about your feelings, or did you try to deny or hide them?

_____

_____

_____

_____

_____

_____

_____

_____

_____

_____

_____

Question: Why were Jonah and John the Baptist each disappointed with God? What are some of the reasons people may feel angry at God? How do our expectations and desires often create doubts about God's character?

_____

_____

_____

_____

_____

_____

_____

_____

_____

_____

Question: Rather than "forgiving" God (since He never fails or does wrong), how should you respond when you are disappointed or angry about what God has or hasn't done?

_____

_____

_____

_____

_____

_____

_____

_____

_____

_____

_____

Action: Study the lives of Job, Jonah, and John the Baptist in Scripture. Why was each man disappointed with God? What was the bigger picture of what God was doing? What lessons might they have learned about God through their disappointment?

_____

_____

_____

_____

_____

_____

_____

_____

Chapter Five Notes

CHAPTER SIX

Practical Steps to Forgiveness

Many of us don't really know what our strengths are because we are driven from the point of insecurity. When you're insecure, you build protective walls around yourself to keep others out, and you become more controlling. Controlling a situation doesn't protect you; rather, it keeps you in even more bondage. The only way to find peace and protection is to release the hurt and thus deprive it of power. The Apostle Paul teaches us to bear with one another:

> *Therefore, as God's chosen people, holy and dearly loved, clothe yourselves with compassion, kindness, humility, gentleness and patience. Bear with each other and forgive one another if any of you has a grievance against someone. Forgive as the Lord forgave you.*
> **—Colossians 3:12–13** (NIV, emphasis mine)

See, you don't have to change everything about yourself or your circumstances. Sometimes you need to just bear with it for a time. That is strength. Unfortunately, we sometimes do a better job at tolerating strangers than we do in our relationships with friends and family. Other people speed, zigzagging through traffic, and it doesn't phase us, but if a family member does those things, we yell. Anybody can forgive a stranger, but it takes a lot of effort to forgive someone whom you know.

Forgiveness takes guts, brains, determination, courage, and love, but you can learn to forgive. Here are some tips:

Why are you hurt? You need to be specific with the person. Tell the person what he or she did and how it hurt you. You cannot bring up everything that has bothered you since you met the person. Instead, you need to get to the root of the one thing that really is upsetting you and work through it.

Don't bring up old hurts and don't be vague. You need to tell the offender what it was he or she did and how it hurt you. Then forgive and let the matter drop.

When you are learning to forgive and to be reconciled to another person, explain what you want. When you address the hurt, articulate what you're expecting. Answer the following questions: Why are we talking about this? What is the outcome that you desire out of this?

Be ready with solutions. I've seen a lot of people who are very good at talking about the problem, but when we ask for a solution, they don't have one. Then we get sucked into that cycle again where someone is hurting but we don't know how to "unhurt" the person. We don't know how to take the hurt out of the person because he or she doesn't even know.

Choose to forgive. If you want to forgive, it's a choice you must make. You may look all fine, but nobody has it all together. There's no one person in this world who has been given everything by God.

When you forgive somebody, learn to verbalize your forgiveness. Don't forgive people secretly, but instead, let them know that the matter is over for you.

Living and Walking in Forgiveness

Living in a spirit of forgiveness means also acting appropriately when you fail. You cannot just ignore what happened and hope that over time, people will forget, and you can move on. You need to ask forgiveness and be reconciled. When the other person involved is a family member, you need to talk to the person and sincerely repent and change your behavior.

If you do something requiring forgiveness in church, you must be humble enough to stand before the congregation and apologize, not just hope that if you stay out of the spotlight people will eventually forget.

In either circumstance, if you just ignore something that happened, then the hurt remains with people, who are waiting until the matter is brought up again. That is why you cannot just ignore a situation where someone is hurt and hope it will go away. I've told you that you need to forgive others who haven't taken the time to apologize;

however, when you've done the wrong thing yourself, you must recognize people may not forgive without an apology. Don't expect someone else—especially a group—to be more spiritually mature than you are yourself.

The Bible says, "But love covers all sins" (Proverbs 10:12 NKJV). The person who demonstrates true love is not the person who acts like he or she is full of the Spirit, and it is not the one who has a story to tell about everyone. Instead, it is the person who is willing to cover over the sins of another.

The more you love, the more you protect. If you have an issue with someone and you call a third person to talk about it, you're exposing someone's sin rather than covering it. Many people are hurt in this way. This can be talking about your pastor, complaining about the director of music when they've made an error, or even sharing what is going on in your personal life.

For example, if someone is going through a divorce, everyone wants to know why. We don't need to know why, because trying to get the person to reveal the reasons doesn't cover the sin. Unfortunately, people will sometimes push, and out of frustration, you may start exaggerating your side of the story and expose the sins. Then the person you spoke to begins to share. You have now started to destroy another person.

Living and walking in forgiveness doesn't expose others and gossip. It tries to focus on the good in other people. If you find that you've been the one exposing the sin, then maybe it is time to change course.

Changing Course

When you see that you've done something wrong, and now you want to do what is right, you may wonder how to cover the offense. What you need to do is learn to conduct some mini-funerals where you bury the offense and get closure. After you've done that, then seek to do some good.

Pray for the other person. In Matthew 5:44, Jesus says to love our enemies. More than that, He says to pray for them. You must learn to pray for your enemies. And then, the next thing to do is to look for reconciliation, if possible.

After you have forgiven someone, then do good. Find ways to bless the person. Don't celebrate when he or she suffers. When your enemy is struggling, don't assume it is God's vengeance for what the person did to you. Don't say to the person, "Oh, you reap what you sow" (Galatians 6:7). Instead, recognize that God loves you as well as that other person. He wants to see both of you happy and blessed. That is why He calls us to forgive—so that we can live in peace with each other. We hurt when we see two people whom we love angry at each other. God loves all of us and wants to see all of us living in peace and joy.

We may remember what someone has done to us, but God doesn't look at us as an individual action, or even as a series of actions. In fact, God doesn't even see you as who you are in one moment in time. He sees you as He created you. God sees you as a completed masterpiece.

Simply because you are missing one piece of a puzzle doesn't mean the whole puzzle doesn't make sense. We live one event and then another, and so we sometimes are caught in a moment and feel like God can no longer use us because of a mistake we made. At other times, there are difficult things we suffer, and we feel broken and alone. There are some things in your life that you can look back on and say, "God, You did that?"

When you change course, you allow God to restart the work in you. Your life may look like a series of zigzags leading to a single destination, but as long as you end up further along from where you started, you are making progress. Try to see the progress and allow God to work through you. Don't focus on what is missing in yourself or in others.

Consider the book of Job in the Bible. He suffered a series of devastating events, despite even God talking positively about him. Furthermore, when Job was at his lowest point, his friends came to try to help him find the sin that had caused the sorrow. At this, Job justified himself and cried out against God. It must have seemed that God had completely forgotten him.

Many of us think that we can't trust God when we don't understand Him or what He is doing. The devil knows that. *The devil cannot stop you from loving God, because that is beyond his reach, but he can put distractions in your relationship with God so that you love God with distrust.*

The devil then extends that distrust to all relationships. If you don't trust somebody in the flesh, whom you can see, that can make it hard to trust God, whom you cannot see. When you're dealing with hard times, the devil will do to you what he did to Eve in the Garden. He will ask things like, "Do you think that God is going to give you the money for your education? No, you need to find a second job." Then he will remind you of the times when you felt that God let you down. He shows you how God didn't give you the second job you applied for. He causes you to focus on that missing puzzle piece.

But God is wanting us to trust Him, and He wonders why we don't. God wants to bless you and give you rest. Instead of asking you to work three jobs to pay for your education, He can give you a single job that pays like four other jobs would. But the devil says, "You cannot trust Him like that. You know what He did last time. You looked like a fool." The devil wants to steal our faith in God's goodness, because he can then derail God's plan. When God is telling us to let go of what we have in order to get something better, all it takes is a bit of doubt from the enemy and we're too afraid to trust God. Without faith, we can miss the wonderful opportunities God is trying to bring us into.

It is too easy to forget that we are God's children and He provides for His children like a good parent does. Jesus said, "I will do whatever you ask in my name, so that the Father may be glorified in the Son" (John 14:13 NIV). Unfortunately, we are convinced that there are things that God just can't do. That is where the enemy gets our attention. Even in the story of Job, where so much doesn't make sense, we can see the power of trusting God and the weakness of the enemy.

Walking in Trust

> *One day the angels came to present themselves before the LORD, and Satan also came with them. The LORD said to Satan, "Where have you come from?" Satan answered the LORD, "From roaming throughout the earth, going back and forth on it." Then the LORD said to Satan, "Have you considered my servant Job? There is no one on earth like him; he is blameless and upright, a man who fears God and shuns evil." "Does Job fear God for nothing?" Satan replied.*
> **—Job 1:6–9** *(NIV)*

In the story of Job, the devil is accusing God, saying that Job only worships God because there is a hedge of protection around Job. The devil is not being accusatory because of our weaknesses, but because of God's blessing on our lives.

The devil knows more about you than you know about yourself. The devil knows that there is a wall around your household, and that your work is blessed, and your possessions will increase. That is why the devil tries to convince us that God won't come through this time. He wants to separate you from the blessing while accusing God of blessing you.

God said to Satan, "Very well, then, everything he has is in your power, but on the man himself do not lay a finger" (Job 1:12 NIV).

There are moments when the devil can request your name. So, suffering will happen, not because you are wrong, but because God has decided to do something without consulting you. You need to understand that there is a divine purpose, even if it includes the pain that you caused, or pain that somebody else caused, or pain that seems to have no origin. There is a purpose for every pain. Job had no idea why, but the pain came.

So, in walked the devil, and he began to destroy things. With the destruction, however, there has always been one person who survived to tell the tale. Whenever you're going through something, the devil will always have one person who knows what you're going through, to make sure everyone else knows, as well. Think about it: Our anxiety doesn't necessarily come from what we're going through, but what we fear other people will think of us. The devil uses gossip. Pain can be handled well when it is not a public thing.

When you're suffering through something, other people tend to talk about it, but remember that what you're going through has nothing to do with your relationship with God. You may think you're sick or enduring something because God is punishing you, and many people in older generations believe that, but that is wrong. The Bible itself says that the days of man are few and full of trouble (Job 14:1). So, when you're going through something, consider keeping your mouth shut so that the devil will have less to work with.

The Bible does say that we can expect life to be challenging, but it also says that God is an ever-present help in trouble (Psalm 46:1). God doesn't promise that we will have a life without affliction, but the Bible does promise that God will deliver us out of all of them. There will be pain and there will be hurt, but God says that we can sleep at night, because He is still awake (Proverbs 3:24; Isaiah 40:28).

Once again, consider the book of Job. People want to focus on the pain that Job endured, but God wants us to focus on the victory that took place at the end. Imagine if Job had been able to simply trust God and remind himself continually that God was on his side. Imagine if Job had born his suffering focusing on the fact that everything would work out in the end. He would not have endured the pain that he did.

Psalm 34:7 says, "The angel of the LORD encamps around those who fear him, and he delivers them" (NIV). So, while we have trouble, there's an angel assigned to each of us. You may see your trouble, but can you imagine what we may have already been delivered from? This is what the devil doesn't say or remind us of, so we suffer, focusing on what isn't happening the way we would like it to happen.

Think about the human body. It is full of bacteria, but there are also white blood cells. Some bacteria are necessary for digestion and for the body to function properly. Without them, we would die. So, if in the physical realm, we need to have some things in our body that seem bad but still help us, isn't it true that the same concept probably applies to our spiritual lives? This is because trouble has led us more to God than blessings have kept us with Him.

It's balance that you need in your life. If you want to be a great man or woman of God, you'll have to go through certain things—and the greater the assignment God has for you, the greater the process of development and the greater the pain. If God is going to use you mightily, the process of development is going to be great and the pain is going to be great, as well, because if you take away the pain, then you can become prideful and may no longer be useful.

When I was a younger preacher, whenever somebody was going through something, I was eager to pray the problem away. I don't do that anymore. Instead, I thank God for every circumstance and what He's going to do through it. God is committed to delivering us from all of our afflictions, but we will still go through many difficult situations. That's made clear in 2 Timothy 3:12, which says: "...all who desire to live godly in Christ Jesus will suffer persecution" (NKJV). This is true of all who desire, not only of all who have accomplished godly living; all of those who simply desire to live godly lives will suffer persecution, but God also looks through the earth to find those He can trust with the challenge.

In Psalm 119:67, David says, "Before I was afflicted I went astray, but now I obey your word" (NIV). David acknowledges that, previously, he had problems. However, he says that it was good for him to be afflicted so that he could learn God's ways and God's laws. There are certain things about God that you can only learn when you are experiencing affliction. David says that he now understood what God wanted from him.

Many people of faith would not be where they are if they hadn't struggled with something. God loves you so much that He trusts you with things that will keep you in the faith. Consider the book of Psalms. Most of David's psalms in the Bible were composed while David was on the run. His pain was turned into ministry through the ages.

Paul is another example of someone who was happy to be afflicted. In fact, in his affliction, he looked around in the poor lighting and saw a Roman soldier. Although Paul was suffering, he saw something good in his situation. He describes the armor of a Roman soldier in the context of the Christian walk and tells us to put on the "whole armor of God" (Ephesians 6:10–18 NKJV).

Don't be so focused on what you're going through that you miss the message that will benefit the world.

Second Corinthians 4:8 teaches us to understand that we may be "hard-pressed on every side, yet not crushed; we are perplexed, but not in despair; persecuted, but not forsaken; struck down, but not destroyed" (NKJV); there are moments when we are struck down, but God promises that there will be no final destruction.

Every morning when you wake up, you have a choice: Either your faith is going to grow, or your fear is going to grow. You have two things to feed each and every day: your faith or fear.

Part of suffering takes place because people don't want to be given direct challenges. We want things to be easy, and we want a nice friendly message to be shared with us. But that isn't how life will always be. This book is meant to teach you how to work with God to handle your suffering and pain when they come. If you don't have something greater than what you're going through, something that you're looking forward to, you will sink. Paul said that the way he handled his suffering was based on the glory that was to come (Romans 5:3). Paul knew that he was suffering, but he refused to whine or to complain. The way we go through an affliction will have a part in determining our victory after that affliction has passed.

The Role of Faith

> *Not only so, but we also glory in our sufferings, because we know that suffering produces perseverance; perseverance, character; and character, hope. And hope does not put us to shame, because God's love has been poured out into our hearts through the Holy Spirit, who has been given to us.*
> **—Romans 5:3–5** *(NIV)*

We also know from Scripture that without faith it is impossible to please God. Faith is the substance of things hoped for (Hebrews 11:1), but we cannot have hope without character, and we cannot have character without perseverance, and we cannot have perseverance without trouble (Romans 5:3–5). So, if you take away your suffering, you'll never have perseverance, which means you will never have character, you will never have hope, and you will never have faith. When you look at it this way, it can be easier to endure the difficult times because you can see a purpose in the pain.

Whenever you're in a situation where you are disappointed with God, take these steps:

- Understand that the same God who led you in will lead you out.

- Realize that God means for you to be where you are. When you do that, it takes away the anxiety and panic, because you're not trying to control God, thinking you are someplace you're not supposed to be.

- Be more concerned about God's glory than your relief.

- View your current crisis as a faith-builder for the future.

When you're suffering, come to church full of thanksgiving. You can do that because of your confidence in God. You are not going to be used by God on the level that you desire to be used if you don't have confidence in God. The confidence is not in you. It's in the promises of God that lead you into His presence and give you His power.

WORKBOOK

Chapter Six Questions

Question: What are some specific steps that will help in confronting an offender and verbalizing your forgiveness? How can going into such a meeting without a plan make things worse?

_____

_____

_____

_____

_____

_____

_____

_____

_____

_____

Question: What does it mean that love covers all sins? How can the spirit of this verse be applied even when you are dealing with a situation that must be reported (i.e., a crime)?

_____

_____

_____

_____

_____

_____

_____

_____

_____

_____

_____

Question: What are some of the positive fruits of suffering in a believer's life?

_____

_____

_____

_____

_____

_____

_____

_____

_____

_____

_____

_____

Action: Plan this week how you can do something good to bless someone who has hurt you or been your enemy. Be sure to pray for them also.

Chapter Six Notes

CHAPTER SEVEN

Forgiving Others

I want to make something clear: all of us have issues with forgiveness. We covered these issues in a previous chapter. For example, we may feel like forgiving someone allows the person to win or keeps him or her from understanding how badly he or she has hurt us. Maybe we're reluctant to forgive because the person shows no remorse. But in this section, we're going to deal with even more. *Forgiveness is not approval or condoning an action. Forgiveness is also not pretending that something didn't happen. It is a way for us to live our lives free from the actions of others.*

In fact, one way to look at the process of forgiveness is like a stretch mark. A stretch mark means change has happened. Nothing makes it go away, and while it might fade, the memory will still be there. Forgiveness is not forgetting or justifying; it is moving beyond that moment. You're not pregnant forever. The stretch mark remains after the pregnancy is over. Likewise, the time of anger and hurt must end, even if some of the memory of the pain will always remain.

Nobody can force you to forgive; it's always a choice. You still have a right to say that someone hurt you and tell the person never to come into your life again. Unfortunately, there's a lot of abuse inflicted on people of faith because they believe that once you forgive, you must forget and then let the person back in your life. You spiritualize your pain. This isn't what is required to forgive.

Likewise, simply because someone went to jail doesn't mean you didn't forgive him or her, or that the person should be allowed to reenter your life as if nothing ever happened. The person may have paid his or her dues to society, but he or she shouldn't be immediately allowed back into your life. Love says that you have to own up for what you've done sometimes. You can pray for a person but also protect yourself. So, don't allow yourself to be abused in the name of forgiveness.

As I said in previous chapters, *forgiveness is not reconciliation.* There are a lot of misunderstandings about this fact, which I will address in more detail in the next chapter. Here, allow me to make this statement with the promise of full explanation later: *Confusing forgiveness and reconciliation is what causes dysfunction.* Forgiveness is not trust. It doesn't mean you will ever again trust the person like you did before. Furthermore, if you have been forgiven by someone, you must be willing to work harder to regain the person's trust.

Let's deal with the three questions we talked about before:

- Have you really forgiven someone if you remember what happened? Yes; since forgiveness is not forgetting, then remembering doesn't mean you have not forgiven.

- Have you really forgiven if you won't let the person back in your life? Yes; since forgiveness is not approval, then standing your ground is not unforgiveness.

- Have you really forgiven if you won't trust the person again? Yes; since forgiveness is not trust, then keeping your guard up is not unforgiveness.

The following verses tell us that when we forgive others, God will forgive us, but if we do not forgive, God won't forgive us, either. *The main reason we forgive is for God's sake.* There is no more important reason to forgive another human being than to do it for God.

And forgive us our debts, as we also have forgiven our debtors.... For if you forgive other people when they sin against you, your heavenly Father will also forgive you. But if you do not forgive others their sins, your Father will not forgive your sins.
—Matthew 6:12, 14–15 *(NIV)*

Yes, a person may have hurt you, and you may have scars, but you must forgive because there are blessings that you are blocking in your own life if you don't bless and forgive the other person. I can only let God know what

I need by what I give to others. So, if you want to be forgiven, you need to forgive also. In the previous chapter, we discussed Job. He went through a terrible trial, but when he repented before God for his attitude and when he forgave his friends, God was able to bless him abundantly.

Another reason we forgive is because the Bible says to tolerate one another. Colossians 3:13 states, "Bear with each other and forgive one another if any of you has a grievance against someone. Forgive as the Lord forgave you" (NIV). We tolerate each other in marriage. We put up with things that we don't like. We're not going to run the other way. You do it on your job, as well. You don't like everybody whom you work with, but you tolerate your coworkers. The paycheck is more important than their foolishness.

We could say it another way. If you can tolerate something, then you don't need to give forgiveness. When you cannot tolerate something, then God says that He gives you the power to forgive. We forgive because we've been forgiven. I may have complaints against you, but since God has forgiven me, I choose to forgive you. Because I have received grace, I owe grace to everyone else around me. So, we forgive for the sake of Christ. Luke 6:37a tells us to judge not and we will not be judged (NKJV). If you don't want to be judged, then don't judge other people. It also says to forgive and we will be forgiven, so if you want to be forgiven, then you first must forgive (Luke 6:37b NKJV).

I personally want to forgive everyone, every time for everything, because I want to receive forgiveness. Remember that reconciliation requires two people, but that's not what I'm talking about here. You can give forgiveness to someone else, even if the person doesn't receive it, because you have made the choice to forgive. You have made the choice to be free.

Great relationships, including great marriages, are made up of great forgivers. There is no marriage that exists where two people have not hurt each other badly but then forgiven each other. People who want a great marriage have to forgive each other. You don't want to date anyone or marry anyone who cannot forgive. If the person you consider marrying has an anger problem, you don't want to be tied to him or her. And if you yourself have these issues, then why would someone want to be married to you?

Psalm 130:3–4 declares: "If you, LORD, kept a record of sins, Lord, who could stand? But with you there is forgiveness, so that we can, with reverence, serve you" (NIV).

Consider what these verses are saying. If God could punish us for all of our wrongdoing, could we stand up and teach anything? Could we go into church and face anyone? It is because of forgiveness that we're able to sing, preach, work, and go to church. We all don't deserve His grace; none of us do.

In Habakkuk, it says that in your anger you should remember mercy (Habakkuk 3:2). We often want mercy when we are guilty, but we want justice when we are innocent. Ephesians 4:32 instructs, "Be kind to one another tenderhearted forgiving one another even as God in Christ forgave you" (NKJV).

Jesus tells us to love each other as He loved us (John 13:34). The standard of loving people is to love as God did. The standard for forgiving people is to forgive as much as God forgave us.

God says that we owe Him the forgiveness that He gave us. 1 Peter 2:21 says, "To this you were called, because Christ suffered for you, leaving you an example, that you should follow in his steps" (NIV).

How are we reflecting Christ? The example is not the person who hurt you. Your example is not even your pastor. Your example is the Holy One, Christ Himself. Even when He was dying on the cross, He took the time to forgive a thief (Luke 23:40–43). This person had never been in church or listened to a sermon before, but he looked at Jesus and said, "Remember me." Consider, too, the woman caught in adultery. All the facts were there. It was true. She had been caught with another man. The Bible says that Jesus stooped to the ground to write in the dirt (John 8:6). When He got up, everyone was gone. We don't need to condone sin, but we should not condemn the sinner (John 8:10–11).

Unforgiveness costs you more than it does to set the person free. People are on antidepressants and in therapy and become alcoholics and drug addicts, all in an effort to push away pain, when what we really need to do is forgive.

Unforgiveness will put weight on you, because you won't sleep; you won't eat; you'll toss and turn in bed all night. If you forgive someone for God's sake, you're doing the best thing you can do for yourself and for the other person, because you are saying to the person that it wasn't about his or her worthiness, but Christ's example. It is about obeying God.

This is also why you need to know what forgiveness is not. You can forgive everyone, every time, when you know what forgiveness is and what forgiveness is not. You're not approving of the hurt when you forgive. You are simply setting the offender free. Forgiveness gives you freedom to move on and to start over again.

When you don't forgive, you are in bondage. The person is always on your mind. Everything will remind you of the person, and you will react and respond to him or her. You need to acknowledge the hurt but change your life, let go, and move on. As you're reading this chapter, the Holy Spirit may have brought some people into your mind. God can help you to forgive them.

Right now, in your mind, imagine God smiling on you as you let them go. And imagine the enemy, the devil himself, frowning. If we can make God smile even when it hurts, we will get more from it than anything we might lose for following God.

Prayer of Forgiveness

Pray this prayer with me:

Father, I want to thank You for what You have done in me as I've read this book. There are people in my mind and heart who have hurt me, whether intentionally or unintentionally. Based on what we learned of Your work so far, I want to forgive them and be forgiven. So, for Your sake, I pray for the Spirit of God to soften my heart so that I can let that person go. I acknowledge the hurt and that there is a scar there. I know I will always remember the offense, but I pray in a very special way that I may gain freedom to move on. I pray for Your gift of freedom. I cannot do this on my own, so I ask You to come in to my life and help me overcome my flesh. In Jesus' name, amen.

WORKBOOK

Chapter Seven Questions

Question: What is the difference between tolerating and forgiving? When is each needed?

_____

_____

_____

_____

_____

_____

_____

_____

_____

_____

_____

Question: Why is forgiveness a key ingredient in every marriage?

_____

_____

_____

_____

_____

_____

_____

_____

_____

Question: Why are you in bondage if you refuse to forgive?

_____

_____

_____

_____

_____

_____

_____

_____

_____

_____

_____

Action: Examine your heart and consider if there are people you need to forgive. Personalize and write out the
prayer of forgiveness at the end of this chapter.

_____

_____

_____

_____

_____

_____

_____

_____

_____

_____

_____

_____

_____

_____

_____

Chapter Seven Notes

CHAPTER EIGHT

Reconciliation

In this chapter, we're going to start transitioning from radical forgiveness to radical reconciliation. Reconciliation is the next level beyond forgiveness. *You can never get reconciled before you forgive.* That is because there's no hope for a relationship getting better if you haven't first forgiven.

The whole Bible hinges on forgiveness and reconciliation. That's why God is not embarrassed to reveal the brokenness of the men and women in the Bible that He shared with us. The greater the assignment, the greater the mess they often made, and the greater the struggle they went through.

You cannot forgive without motivation. It's beyond us as human beings to forgive without motivation. There are four things that motivate us to forgive and to take things to another level:

We forgive in order to obey God. Forgiveness is a command from God. We must forgive. If God is not the reason, then the reason is not good enough. If God is not the reason, you're going to be hurt again. Here are some reasons why we forgive:

We forgive in order to delight God. We want to see a smile on God's face, hoping to please Him. So, I don't forgive because you deserve it. Nobody deserves forgiveness; that's why you cannot earn it.

We choose to forgive in order to bring glory to God. Forgiveness is a choice.

When you choose to forgive, you help fulfill God's mission of reconciliation. God is depending on us assisting Him in the divine mission of reconciling the world to Himself. We give people a little taste of heaven when we forgive them. You are fulfilling God's master plan for the human race.

> Now the serpent was more crafty than any of the wild animals the LORD God had made. He said to the woman, "Did God really say, 'You must not eat from any tree in the garden'?"
> —*Genesis 3:1 (NIV)*

In this story, we learn a few things that teach us about sin, forgiveness, and reconciliation.

During the exchange between Eve and the serpent, only Eve and the serpent are recorded. We know Adam was there, because Eve gave some of the fruit to him. God knew everything that happened, because He is omniscient.

Adam and God listened as the serpent twisted and misrepresented God's instructions.

The devil focused Eve on what she might be missing, rather than all she had. The Bible tells us that she looked at the tree and saw that it was good for food, pleasant to the eye, and desirable for gaining wisdom (Genesis 3:6 NIV). What you need to understand is that she started out wishing for things beyond what she had experienced, simply by focusing on the tree. How do you know that something is good for you before you even eat it? Sin makes the mysterious appealing, and the world tells you that the tree was good. She didn't know that. She didn't listen to God. She indulged in what she thought would make her feel better and not what God commanded.

Nothing will ever affect your life without you giving it your attention. Unforgiveness looks appealing and seems like something you'd like to experience, but it leads to the path of death. By turning away from the temptation to hold on to anger, you can forgive. Not only that, but because God commands us to forgive, you can forgive everybody, every time, for everything as long as you don't give attention to the details of the pain.

You can see this in childbirth. When a woman gives birth to a baby, she may say she'll never do it again, but then she usually has a second and sometimes a third. Why does she do this? Because she's no longer focused on the pain, but rather she's focused on the baby and the joy the baby brings. Since she changes her focus, her priorities change. She sees the pain of labor as a small price to pay in exchange for the joy of a child.

It is the same way with your pain. If you give attention to what hurt you, that's what you'll magnify. Whatever you focus on—whether good or bad—will flourish, and it will gain the power to control you.

Unforgiveness is like investing $1 million when you're only going to get a $10 profit.

It doesn't matter how much you've been hurt in a relationship, you also have a contributing factor to the demise of a broken relationship. Eve ate the fruit and became one with all of her desires, but in the process, she broke the relationship she had with God. Then, she offered the fruit to Adam, and he ate it, too. In the process, Adam's relationship with God was destroyed, too (Genesis 3:6–10). When you mess up, you mess up other people, because messed-up people mess up people.

There are three types of silence whenever something is going wrong:

The first is a sinful silence that just lets whatever is happening happen. Think about the people in the story of the Good Samaritan who just left the person on the side of the road to die (Luke 10:25–37). Many relationships are broken because of sinful silence; instead of talking to God, they're talking about God. When we start talking about people, watch out, because it means that we are not addressing the One who can fix it. Instead of reconciling, we are gossiping.

The second is the redemptive silence. That's God's silence all the time. When God is silent when you are messing up, His silence is usually the seed to wake you up. That's why we should never ignore God when He is silent. Grace is the redemptive silence of God when we are messing up. Grace means that even though Eve and the snake were talking, God was quiet. Even today, God's there, silently hoping that somehow in the back of your head, you're going to remember to seek Him and choose not to sin.

The third is punitive silence. Don't keep silent when you are angry. There are people going to hell because those who love them just stayed silent. When you are hurt, if you stay quiet, it will make matters worse and reconciliation will never begin.

Many times, reconciliation doesn't happen without the offended party initiating the conversation. That could be because you don't know that you've hurt someone else until the person approaches you, or because you have so much pride that you feel you were justified in hurting the other person. The one who was right always has the power to fix the one who was wrong. That is why God says that if you are strong, you should come down to the level of the weaker one (1 Corinthians 8:9, 10:24).

Maybe you feel like it is always you who is initiating forgiveness, even when you didn't cause the break in the relationship. Eve was looking for wisdom, but she didn't seek it from God. God wanted them to live in a continual innocent state. He wanted them to live in His goodness and in His perfection. Eve sought the wisdom that God did not want them to have. Even though it was Eve who hurt God, God initiated the restoration of the relationship.

The offender will rarely fix the relationship. That is because when you're guilty, if you come to apologize, the offended party might be suspicious. Guilt also draws us away. Adam and Eve hid under leaves (Genesis 3:7). But that is why, when God came, He came at the right time, in the right place, and with the right tone. It's not only what you say, but it's your tone that counts. God came with love and with a plan for Adam and Eve to be reconciled to Him.

However, reconciliation has to begin with you being honest about where you are. It's like with GPS: you have to start where you are now. You cannot begin where you were five days ago or where you will be three days from now. The only way to get to where you're going is to begin where you are now.

God never focused on what broke the relationship, but He focused on the Seed of the woman, who was going to restore the relationship. Galatians 3:16 tells us: "The promises were spoken to Abraham and to his seed. Scripture does not say, 'and to his seeds,' meaning many people, but 'and to your seed,' meaning one person, who is Christ" (NIV).

Christ had already been slain before the foundation of the world (Revelation 13:8). The forgiveness that you give when you're trying to reconcile with someone is a forgiveness you had before the relationship was ever broken. The prayer that gets you through difficult times is not the prayer that you pray when you're in the middle of them. It is the prayer you prayed before things started happening. Sometimes I tell God that I don't know how to help people, because when people are already in a situation, it's usually too late to cry out. Whatever you're praying prepares you for the next thing. It's the prayer before the storm that sustains you in the storm, and the prayer in the storm prepares you for when you're out of the storm.

When man brought sin into the world, God was silent, but He had a plan of redemption. He was already preparing to reconcile people to Him. God essentially said, "You blew it, but there's a Man, the Seed of the woman, who is going to fix it" (Genesis 3:14–15)

This is how God fixes it. Don't be confused. This is not the seed of a man. All of us were born from the seed of a man. Jesus was the only Man who was born by a woman. The seed of the woman, Eve, is owning up for her wrong, and when God speaks, Eve is now the solution. God is not saying that He's going to punish her because she ate the fruit first. He says that there is a baby that would come through her and that a virgin would give birth to a child (Isaiah 7:14).

Reconciliation of Broken Relationships

This is how God brought redemption and the reconciliation of His relationship with us, but how do we reconcile with someone else? First, if you are the offended person, when you go to reconcile, do not put the other person in a corner. Don't make others feel bad. You need to give them a way out. Be gracious. Jesus says in Matthew 18 that if someone has offended you, don't tell the world; simply go to that person and talk to him or her (Matthew 18:15). Preserve the person's dignity. God knows how to deal with the situation. He tells us to go to the person alone and talk to him or her. If the individual doesn't listen, then ask a brother or sister in Christ to join you (Matthew 18:16). That person shouldn't even know why he or she is going until he or she gets there and hears it the first time. Don't bad-mouth the person the whole way. You should only talk to the offender. If the offender still doesn't listen, then there is a process, but you start here (Matthew 18:17). This is God's plan.

When a relationship is broken, it doesn't matter who caused it, because everybody gets hurt. There is something very interesting in the creation story that you may have missed. God declares that everything is good, but then He says that it is not good for man to be alone (Genesis 1:31; 2:18). How is this possible? You can't be alone with God? There is a development that never flourishes when it is only you and God and no other flesh-and-blood human being.

Relationships between people are important. One famous relationship is described in the story of Jacob and Esau, which starts in Genesis 33. These brothers had a broken relationship before they were even out of their mother's womb. The Bible says that they were fighting in the womb as two warring nations, and God had chosen one over the other.

Neither brother was particularly good. Jacob was a thief. He stole from his brother. He stole from Laban. Then he married Rachel, who was also a thief and ended up stealing all of the idols from her father. Esau married foreign women who made his mother frustrated. God doesn't look at who we are in the beginning. He knows who we can become when we reconcile with Him and with each other.

In the story of the reconciliation of Jacob and Esau, Jacob had run away many years earlier after stealing his brother's birthright. He was now returning to his home country. He heard that Esau was coming with a large group of people, about four hundred. He was certain that this meant that Esau was going to war against Jacob to get revenge. So, Jacob sent the women ahead, and he stayed on the other side of the river that night. He lay down and during the night was attacked by a man with whom he wrestled all night. It wasn't until morning that he realized that the Man was God Himself.

He must have thought that it was Esau sneaking up on him at night, so he was afraid and fought with everything he had. But, in the morning, God asked Jacob what his name was; it was Jacob. God responded by saying, "From now on your name shall be called Israel" (Genesis 32:27–28). This is reconciliation. God said that He was changing his name from Jacob to Israel because he had fought with God and prevailed.

Although Jacob had wrestled all night, he still had not conquered his fear, which was facing his brother, Esau. When God was speaking with Jacob (Israel), He was assuring him that he already had the victory in advance. He told Jacob that even before he met his brother.

However, Jacob didn't fully trust that promise. That is likely because he had been used to saying whatever he needed to say to get his way all his life. He also married a woman who would lie and steal to get her way. He had lived in Laban's house and had been lied to on his wedding night. He didn't really have any context of people who were truthful and honest.

Therefore, when Jacob crossed over, he still bowed down full of fear. Esau ran to meet Jacob, because suddenly, for the first time ever, he missed his brother. This is the key to getting reconciliation when a relationship is broken. It all starts with God. If God is not in the process of reconciliation, it is not going to work. You cannot reconcile human beings without God, because life has a way of dividing relationships.

God is the glue for people of broken relationships. Unfortunately, sometimes we want the blessing without the Blesser. The true blessing is knowing God and knowing Jesus, because this gives you eternal life. We cannot have any blessing without being in relationship with Him. That means first cleansing the sin away that has separated us from God.

Jesus is the only means to reconciliation with God and with each other. One reason we need to push the Great Commission (Matthew 28:16–20) is because there are some relationships in our lives that will never be restored without God. If Christ is not a part of the package, no matter what you do, even if you're coming to church together, the relationship will not be reconciled. To achieve real reconciliation, you have a true relationship with God first.

We were enemies of God (Romans 5:10). God was on the other side, and Jesus became the bridge. Reconciliation can only happen through Him. If you take Christ out of the picture, nothing happens. But when He comes in, relationships get better.

Too many people want the fruits of knowing Him without knowing Him. It's like a woman who gets pregnant and has a baby and then ignores the father. Even though the father was a part of making the baby, she is no longer interested in the husband, and she may not even trust her husband with the baby. It's that way with God. We can become so addicted to His blessings that we are willing to push away our relationship with Him. As long as we have good health, then we don't care whether or not God is in our lives.

Jesus was the opposite of this. He was more concerned about the inner availability of God and His presence than the blessings. When He felt God move away, Jesus cried out, asking why He had been forsaken. That's because Jesus had never lived without God before. He didn't care about anything else. Losing that relationship with God caused Him to actually cry out. Unfortunately, some of us are perfectly content with money or even with our friends, and we don't really care whether or not the presence of God is there, as long as the music is right.

> *All this is from God, who reconciled us to himself through Christ and gave us the ministry of reconciliation: that God was reconciling the world to himself in Christ, not counting people's sins against them. And he has committed to us the message of reconciliation.*
> **—2 Corinthians 5:18–19** *(NIV)*

Look at what this tells us. All things belong to God, and through Christ, He has given us the ministry of reconciliation. So, in other words, God brought us back to

Himself and He gave us the power to pass it on. When I reconcile with you, it's not because you first came to me, but because God was there and empowered me to extend His reconciliation through me to you.

What Does Reconciliation Look Like?

Godly reconciliation is a permanent thing. If you say you want to reconcile, it means you're about to fix the problem and you will be part of the process until it's done. Here is a list of what reconciliation means:

Reconciliation means you are rescued and transferred. Reconciliation goes beyond freedom to inclusion. Colossians 1:13 says that Jesus "delivered us from the domain of darkness and brought us into the kingdom of the Son he loves" (NIV). It's not your hate for the devil, but your love for God that accomplishes the mission. Some of us are addicted to how much we hate the devil, but the only thing that can hurt the devil is your love for God. So, when you are working to reconcile, it isn't just about getting past the hurt. That is forgiveness. You need God in order to have reconciliation at all. In order to be reconciled, you have to praise God and trust Him with the person. When you see that person in church or singing in the choir, you won't judge them or avoid them. You will praise God with them.

Reconciliation means that you also have forgiveness of your sins in Christ. You cannot appreciate the gift of reconciliation until you celebrate the benefits of your relationship with God and the knowledge that God has forgiven you in the first place. The book of Colossians has powerful principles in it about our relationship with God. It says that through His blood we have forgiveness of sins (Colossians 1:14 KJV). We don't have redemption outside of Christ. It's not enough to be a good person.

A lot of people don't want to hear this message. The church is weak because people only want self-help presentations, but what you're looking for can only be found in Christ.

When you are in Christ, reconciliation means you have peace with God. Colossians 1:20 says that Christ reconciles all things to Himself. When you are reconciled to God, you have peace with Him: you have the peace of God, and you have peace from God. That's why the Bible says that when you are faced with a situation that may cause you to worry, you should be anxious for nothing (Philippians 4:6). He will give us what we need (Philippians 4:19). We will receive the peace of God, which surpasses all understanding.

This doesn't mean the situation is not bad. To the contrary, it means the peace of God will give you sleep in the midst of your worst circumstances. Reconciliation makes the offenders talk comfortably and forget they were ever offended. Now you know that when somebody hurts you, it is possible to be reconciled. I want you to understand this, but I want you to know that it may take everything out of you to trust God with the situation.

Let me give you an illustration in the natural. Have you ever flown somewhere? It's crazy for you to say that, because on your own you cannot fly, right? It's the *plane* that flies. In the same way, certain things are only possible to do in Christ. If you are not in Christ, you cannot forgive or reconcile, just like you cannot "fly" unless you're in a plane. But when you sit inside of a plane, you can claim all the benefits of that plane.

Let me take the analogy a step further. Have you noticed that you can sleep on a flight? You've never met the pilot and you don't know whether he or she is trustworthy or if he or she is on drugs, but you can take a nap on a plane, trusting that you will land safely at your destination. If you can do this in the natural, you should also be able to do it in the spiritual. When you are in Christ, you can take a nap and still get to where you're going, because you are no longer the one controlling the situation. Because you believe in Him, you have the benefit of the cross.

Reconciliation means that Christ initiated and pursued a relationship with you. You had nothing to do with it. You were running away from Christ, but He fell in love with you first. No verse in the Bible says that you're lovable. It says that you're the apple of God's eye (Zechariah 2:8; Psalm 17:8), but it doesn't say there's anything lovable about you.

In the earthly realm, if you were to be reconciled to somebody, it is the offended person, not the offender, who must initiate the relationship and pursue it, because the offender has lost the right to deserve a relationship with the person whom they offended. No matter how much we want to have a relationship with God, as human beings, none of us has it in us to go back to God and ask for a relationship, because we were separated from God by our sin. Thank God the Bible says that love keeps no record of wrongs (1 Corinthians 13:5). That is a difficult verse for me to understand, because my flesh always wants to remind me what I have done wrong, but when I repent, God washes it away and doesn't remember my sin anymore. He restores His relationship with me and then commands me to do the same for others.

As with all things, however, timing is crucial. God did not immediately restore mankind when Adam and Eve sinned in the Garden. There was a period of time that passed and a series of steps that had to take place. Furthermore, although He offered reconciliation, only those who accepted the terms were restored. In this next chapter, I will share with you the importance of the right timing and the danger of premature reconciliation.

WORKBOOK

Chapter Eight Questions

Question: Does reconciliation typically start with the offender or the offended? Why?

_____

_____

_____

_____

_____

_____

_____

_____

_____

_____

_____

Question: How did God demonstrate reconciliation after Adam and Eve sinned?

_____

_____

_____

_____

_____

_____

_____

_____

_____

_____

_____

Question: What does our reconciliation with God through Christ look like? What blessings are a part of this reconciliation?

_____

_____

_____

_____

_____

_____

_____

_____

_____

_____

_____

_____

Action: Read the principles of Matthew 18. Ask your pastor or one of the leaders of your church to describe (without identifying details) a situation in which they put these steps into action. How should individual church members handle matters between themselves?

Chapter Eight Notes

_____

_____

_____

_____

_____

_____

_____

_____

_____

_____

_____

_____

_____

_____

_____

_____

_____

_____

_____

_____

_____

CHAPTER NINE

Premature Reconciliation

How can you tell if reconciliation is premature? The key is whether or not you have addressed the issue that caused the separation in the first place. If you haven't dealt with that, you're going to hit the same wall again eventually. That's normally what happens with us when we get into these relationships. We jump in before we understand the price that the relationship will cost us.

In the Bible, the fruit of the Spirit is the evidence that the Holy Spirit is present in your life (Galatians 5:22). Likewise, there are fruits in a person's life or in a relationship that can tell you whether the time is right for reconciliation. Now let's examine five fruits that will let you know if reconciliation is real or premature.

The first fruit of premature reconciliation is a spirit of justifiable resentment. That means resentment that is qualified. If you still feel resentment toward the person, then you must first step back and forgive before you can move to a place of reconciliation.

The second fruit occurs after you believe you have forgiven somebody, if you begin to feel arrogant entitlement. This is entitlement that makes you feel above another person, like you are super spiritual or better than others. If you have this, you must repent and let that go.

David had arrogant entitlement. We can see it when the prophet came to him and talked about the man who had one sheep and he cared for that sheep (2 Samuel 12:1–13). The rich man had many sheep, but instead of slaughtering one of his own sheep for a meal, he stole the only sheep of the poor man. David said that man must die, and the prophet of God then said, "You are that man." All of us can be arrogantly entitled when you hear a story in the third person and you end up instead sending yourself to hell. Why should it be okay for you yourself to do something that you condemn in your enemy?

The third fruit that lets you know you are facing a premature reconciliation is stubborn resistance. Stubborn resistance is when someone resists everything you suggest simply because you suggested it. When a relationship is broken, you may want it to work, but your sensitivity is heightened. If you are trying to hold someone under guilt by letting the person know that you're always watching him or her, then you are not ready to reconcile.

The fourth fruit is blind ignorance. Blind ignorance is refusing to see the truth about a person.

The fifth fruit is disconnected isolation. This fruit is produced when disconnection and no desire to connect flourish.

If you see any of these fruits in your reconciliation, then you need to step back to the place of forgiveness and allow God to work in and through you so that you can then try to reconcile. There are certain things that even in our own human relationships can only function as we focus on God. *Remember, forgiveness, reconciliation, and even restoration aren't about what people did to us, but about what God can do through us*

The problem we have is that we always want to know how to please people instead of focusing on how we can please God. If you're trying to please people, you'll fail all the time, but when you try to please God, you're going to please most of the people all of the time. That is why, whatever you do, you need to do it to the glory of God. Remember that all of us are human. Simply because we believe in God doesn't mean that we've become a "little God."

> *Remain in me, as I also remain in you. No branch can bear fruit by itself; it must remain in the vine. Neither can you bear fruit unless you remain in me.*
> *—John 15:4 (NIV)*

There are three important lessons in this text. First, you have to choose intentionally to abide in Christ and to let Christ abide in you. Then, you have the mind of Christ (1 Corinthians 2:16). That's focusing on "whatever things are true, whatever things are noble, whatever things are just, whatever things are pure, whatever things are lovely, whatever things are of good report..." (Philippians 4:8). Think on these things instead of focusing on the earthly things. We must focus on what is heavenly. The only thing that makes that possible is when we abide in Christ and He abides in us. And once those two things happen, Christ through us bears fruit.

So, when we abide in Christ and He abides in us, we still don't bear fruit, but rather, Christ bears fruit through us. In this chapter, the fruit we are talking about is reconciliation. In other words, when I am in Christ and He is in me, Christ, through me, reconciles the relationship.

Colossians 3:13 instructs us: "Bear with each other and forgive one another if any of you has a grievance against someone. Forgive as the Lord forgave you" (NIV).

There is a price for reconciliation, such as bearing with one another. In previous chapters we talked about forgiving one another and bearing with one another. Sometimes after we forgive another person, we want to remind the person of what he or she did to us. While your carnal nature may feel better doing this, the primary recipient of the benefits of forgiveness is not the one who gives forgiveness, so doing this only steals the joy of forgiving.

Another thing that leads to premature reconciliation is when we think reconciliation is silence on things that we don't like. There's a difference between peacekeeping and peacemaking. Many people are peacekeepers because they are quiet, but when we are quiet on something that we should say something about, resentment starts to build up. And when resentment is fully pregnant, it gives birth to hate. Any relationship only works by grace. That's why you shouldn't take any person's words to heart too much. Even people who clap their hands for you on one thing may not like something else you say. Then they may choose to focus on that one thing that you disagree about instead of all the different things you do agree about. That is why we need to forgive each other and tolerate each other above all things.

What Must We Do?

Bear with each other and forgive one another if any of you has a grievance against someone. Forgive as the Lord forgave you. And over all these virtues put on love, which binds them all together in perfect unity.

Let the peace of Christ rule in your hearts, since as members of one body you were called to peace. And be thankful. Let the message of Christ dwell among you richly as you teach and admonish one another with all wisdom through psalms, hymns, and songs from the Spirit, singing to God with gratitude in your hearts. And whatever you do, whether in word or deed, do it all in the name of the Lord Jesus, giving thanks to God the Father through him.
—Colossians 3:13–17 (NIV)

To forgive and tolerate others, you must first *put on love* (Colossians 3:14). You cannot reconcile with anyone whom you don't love. I don't care how many sermons you've heard, how much you read your Bible, or how many books you've read, if you don't love a person, you may smile at them, but you will never reconcile.

Second, *let the peace of God rule in your heart* (Colossians 3:15). There are certain things that can only be worked out when the peace of God is ruling in your heart. God's emotions don't fluctuate like ours do. He is constant. That's the kind of peace you need in your life, so that when you go to a person for reconciliation, you can be calm. You see, you cannot control anyone. One thing that makes Christian marriages sometimes worse than secular marriages is that Christians try to spiritualize their pain. We take other people's decisions and own them as if we had some kind of control over those situations. The only thing you have on your side is the peace of God ruling in your heart.

Third, the Word of Christ must *dwell in you richly* (Colossians 3:16). The key word there is *richly*. This is not just on the surface, when you read through the Scriptures and nothing changes. It's not done by reading through the Bible and cherry-picking your favorite parts. You can't go to the mountaintop with that. The Word of God must become your joy. That way, you can say, "It is written."

The expression "It is written" frees you, because you are standing on the Word of God and God's Word has the power to make things happen. If you live your life based on what you think, and if your opinion is what rules you, there are certain relationships that will never work. For example, the Word of God says to love your enemies (Matthew 5:43-48). You can't do that on your own, but if you let the Word of God rule in your heart, then God can love your enemies through you.

You don't forgive people because they are good. If they become good, that's even better, but the real reason for forgiveness is the Word of God. So, you're forgiving others because you want your relationship with God to be good. If it benefits the other person, praise God for it. If it makes you feel better, praise God for it. But the primary reason you're doing it is because you want Him to smile on you.

Let's keep looking at this verse. Now that I have forgiven, and now that I have put on love, and now that the peace of God is ruling in my heart and the Word of Christ is dwelling richly in my life, *God calls me to begin to do things.* Whatever you do, do it as if you're doing it for God. In other words, whatever you do should become an act of worship. Imagine dealing with your enemy as an act of worship. Imagine dealing with your children as an act of worship.

That's what Romans 12:1 says, that worship becomes your reasonable service (NKJV). I'm not talking about doing it because you fear God, but, rather, doing it because you love God. There's a difference between doing something out of love and doing something out of fear. Many people go to church because they are afraid of God and His punishment, but when you come to church because you love God, something changes in you. You become a spiritually mature Christian. Faith is not blind. Faith is intelligent.

The Bible is a story of restoration. God set the example for us in the body of Christ so that we could forgive and be reconciled. Just like in the Scriptures, however, there is a proper time and a proper way to reconcile with others. Once you've forgiven the person who hurt you and you've allowed the pain, anger, and other negative feelings to fade, then you can be reconciled to the person. That means you can begin to rebuild the relationship. The final step of this process is restoration, which is where we will turn now.

Chapter Nine Questions

Question: What are some attitudes that indicate premature reconciliation?

_____

_____

_____

_____

_____

_____

_____

_____

_____

_____

_____

Question: What spiritual attitudes are needed for reconciliation to take place?

_____

_____

_____

_____

_____

_____

_____

_____

_____

_____

Question: How is reconciliation an act of worship?

_____

_____

_____

_____

_____

_____

_____

_____

_____

_____

_____

Action: Study the story of David and Absalom in 2 Samuel 13–18. How did premature reconciliation actually make the relationship worse? What principles can you learn from this failed reconciliation?

_____

_____

_____

_____

_____

_____

_____

_____

_____

_____

Chapter Nine Notes

_____

_____

_____

_____

_____

_____

_____

_____

_____

_____

_____

_____

_____

_____

_____

_____

_____

_____

_____

_____

_____

CHAPTER TEN

Restoration

We live in a broken world full of sin. Therefore, there are times when we fall victim to the sins of others. In the Bible, there are many stories of people who had to pay the price for the sin and unbelief of others. We already talked about Joshua and Caleb spending forty years in the desert because of the ten spies who gave a wicked report (Numbers 32:13). All of us have paid the price for the sin of Adam and Eve (Romans 5:12). However, knowing this doesn't make it easier for us when we feel we are being given a raw deal due to the mistakes of others.

Mephibosheth of Lo-debar

There is a story in the Bible of a man who lost a great inheritance due to the sins of his family, was crippled due to an accident caused by someone else, but then was restored because of a person with a forgiving heart and good character.

In 2 Samuel 9, David was looking for someone to bless from the house of Saul because of his friend Jonathan. At this point, David had been the king for some time, but he had always honored Saul as God's anointed king. Furthermore, Saul's son Jonathan had protected David from his father. It is in this context that David asked whom he could bless from Saul's house (2 Samuel 9:1).

In David's castle, a man named Ziba said that he knew where a descendant of Saul lived. This descendant was named Mephibosheth. David wanted to honor his friend's memory, and no doubt he was excited to hear of this person. However, Ziba quickly added that Mephibosheth was lame. This was an important fact to know, because David had made it illegal for any blind or lame person to come into the city of Jerusalem. While by today's standards that may seem cruel, David had done this because when he took the city from the heathens, they had said that even the blind and lame could destroy him (2 Samuel 5:6). Out of anger, David had made the law (2 Samuel 5 6–8). Despite his own law, David summoned the descendant of Saul, Mephibosheth, in order to bless him.

Mephibosheth was lame because his feet had been broken. In 2 Samuel 4, Saul and his sons were killed at war. Mephibosheth was just a young child, and when his nurse scooped him up in an effort to save him, she fell, dropped him, and his feet were broken. It was not Mephibosheth's fault that he was lame, but now he was in danger for his life and would be permanently unable to run. When David sent for Mephibosheth, he was living in exile in a place called Lo-debar.

Consider this: After a period of time in which Mephibosheth lived outside of his inheritance, God encouraged someone to seek him out and bring him into a time of blessing. David wanted to give grace and mercy to someone who didn't necessarily deserve it. This man hadn't earned what David was offering him; he only received it because he was associated with David's friend Jonathan.

It's important to note that when the time of this man's blessing came, someone knew who he was and where he was. No matter what happens in life, there is always somebody who knows where you are. That person may not tell you that he or she knows, but the person does know, and at the right time, whether good or bad, your location will be exposed. That's why it's important to be doing God's work.

Once Mephibosheth was brought to him, David invited him to eat at his table every day. Mephibosheth had lived in that hard place for so long that he referred to himself as a "dead dog." Do you ever feel so beat down and defeated that you would call yourself that? Choices his family had made and the mistakes of those who had been sent to care for him had broken him and stolen his blessings. He now lived below his station, and he felt even lower than that.

However, it was time for God's deliverance. Not only was Mephibosheth well provided for, but he was even to eat at David's table. Furthermore, David restored his family lands to him and assigned people to work the lands and to give Mephibosheth the profit.

Lessons from Mephibosheth's Life

Maybe you have a condition that someone else is responsible for causing. It's not necessarily that someone meant to hurt you. In fact, in this story, the nurse was trying to help. Her intentions were good, but her mistake was permanent. Maybe you've made a genuine mistake that's caused results that can never be fixed. Something is now in place that will always remind you of what you did. This story shows you that restoration is still possible.

Not everybody who struggles is struggling due to his or her own sin. Some people are struggling with things over which they had no control. We punish the woman who wanted to save her marriage, but whose husband left her. She kept the faith, but he left. Yet we still stigmatize her.

Even good intentions can produce a bad outcome. Many Christians have good intentions. They go to church, but they don't grow spiritually. They sit and listen to a few messages by the pastor, but they don't let the words change them. Hell will be full of people with good intentions.

Furthermore, bad people all typically have good intentions. A bad person can defend their actions, because in their own head, what they're doing is a good thing. That is also why God says that faith without works is dead (James 2:20). Faith can only be seen by your works. You may have good faith, but just because you have faith doesn't mean that it is alive. You can have dead faith; it is still faith. Mephibosheth's nurse wanted to save the baby, thinking that he might even regain the throne someday, but her good intentions damaged him permanently.

You may be a person who looks at what's going on in your life and sees that what happened wasn't your fault, but people still have no mercy for you. That's why I love Jesus more than I love people. Just as Jesus disobeyed the Law of Moses by touching the lepers to heal them (Matthew 8:1–4), God will take us to a place that is uncomfortable.

Mephibosheth grew up as a descendant of the king, until one day he was whisked away on a horse with broken feet, crippled and lame and hidden away. Then, when Mephibosheth was an adult, royal guards knocked on his door. When they called for him, he figured he was as good as dead.

And then Mephibosheth entered the castle. He was in the right place, but in the wrong condition. He knew he had royal blood in his veins, but he was limping in, and then he fell on his face. Mephibosheth was showing respect to the king because he didn't know why he was there. This is how we need to be, as well.

David did not address the descendant of Saul as "royalty," but by his first name. We can't allow ourselves to be caught up in titles and feel like spirituality is all about names. Cleaning toilets is an act of God. It's holy to clean the church. There are some people doing nothing to help because they are only focusing on what they don't have rather than what they do have. You can't serve God out of what you don't have.

Mephibosheth was the only lame man above the law in Jerusalem. That is grace. Whenever people could hear the clicks of him coming with his crutches, they knew it was Mephibosheth. The condition that had made him hide became the condition that ultimately testified.

Sitting around King David's table were mighty men, handsome princes, and beautiful princesses. There was the attractive King David with his ability to write songs and his love for God. There were people of beauty like Absalom and Amnon. And then there was Mephibosheth, with his obvious physical disability.

The one who appeared worse off than everybody else in the room was the one who was cleaner than everybody else in the room. He was now sitting in his right position, only in the wrong condition. That's the humbling favor of God.

When God gives you favor, He always leaves something in your life to remind you that you didn't get there easily. It wasn't easy for you to get there, and you don't qualify to be there. You don't deserve to be there, but you're there anyway—because of His favor.

God has a way of working with what we can do and what we have, rather than focusing on what we can't do or don't have. I don't worry about people who don't attend my church and simply minister to those whom God does send.

If you can't pray for an hour a day, can you pray for thirty seconds? God asked Moses for what he had in his hand (Exodus 4:2). It was nothing more than a dead stick, but with that stick, God brought life into a snake. We just need to give God something to work with, and that begins with our obedience.

Restoration is the ultimate goal for God and for those of us who love God. I'm tired of excuses. No excuse is good enough for your relationship with God to be sacrificed. Wimpy Christians quit when a little setback occurs. You've got to be faithful until you die. When I see people being weak, not having a weakness but *being weak*, it makes me sad, and I'm not even your God. He's been so faithful to you. Have you ever stopped to think why you are still alive and have the blessings that you have?

Some of us are so addicted to people that we miss God. We may go to church and know the sermon is for us. We may want to get things straight with God, but we refuse to go to the altar because we are too concerned about the opinions of others. Who cares what the other people think?

Not everyone in church is going to be blessed. I used to say that all of us are blessed, but we're not. Some are cursed, and others are blessed. You are blessed based on your relationship with God. Simply because you came to church smelling good doesn't mean you're going to be blessed. You have got to be willing and ready to love Him to get His blessing. You must be willing to get uncomfortable to receive His blessing.

Remember the man whom Jesus healed on the Sabbath. He told him to take up his bed and walk (John 5:8 NKJV). This was significant, because this man would have been the only person carrying a bed on the Sabbath. Sometimes, God doesn't want you to talk about what He has done; you just need to show it. The issue was the man carrying his bed, because he was the only man carrying that testimony. Some of you are not ready to be blessed by God because you are fighting your own condition. You don't want to look like what you used to be, and yet the power of God is only greater when you reveal what you used to be, compared to what you are now.

It's About Reconciliation

Now, what does all of this mean to us? It's about reconciliation. If you're going to reconcile with anybody, you're going to have to change your rules. David had to change the rules for one person in order for reconciliation to take place.

You cannot have a relationship with God without the initiation of God (John 6:44). Just as Mephibosheth was summoned by the king, we are also summoned by the king. Don't ask Jesus to make you good—that's a terrible prayer. It means that you think you have to be good to be loved by God. See, our problem is that we're punishing people for where they are coming from, when their destiny is not where they're coming from but where they're going to. That's why Paul said that he was forgetting what's behind and pressing to the future (Philippians 3:13).

Not everything wrong in your life is because you caused it yourself. There are children who are behaving badly because their parents divorced. The divorce was not the children's fault. They did not have a part in that decision, but God says that He has plans for those children, plans for their future and hope (Jeremiah 29:11).

Each morning when I wake up, I pick up my gallon of water and look at the word *recycle*. It's my morning sermon, because if man can take a dirty old thing and repurpose it, then how much more can God? He says that any man in Christ is a new creature (2 Corinthians 5:17 KJV). He can make us a brand-new creation, as well. Don't give up on God, and don't define yourself by your bad past and your bad choices. There's nothing glorious in your past. I don't care whether it was bad or good; it's over. Don't live in your past; do new things for God daily.

Maybe you feel left out. All your life, you may have been fighting different things, but you're here reading this now and God is talking to you today. Today, you want real reconciliation with God and deliverance. You may stay in the condition you're in, but you want a new assignment for your pain. You want to testify that God is able, and He is good. God's table is defined by the King who is calling, and Jesus is even greater than David.

The End of the Matter

We have talked about forgiveness, relationships, reconciliation, walking away, and staying true. This is the end of the matter. God is more than able to walk with you through this process. Your relationship with Him cannot be replaced. That is why, without God, certain things would never happen. When you seek to please God, human relationships take care of themselves, but for this to happen, we need to trust Him. That means relinquishing control over the situation.

The problem is, we give God control and then two weeks later we feel He is taking too long, and we try to take our control back. You may think the devil is messing with you when it's actually *you* trying to take over the role of God. You need to quit trying to control things and let God control what is happening. When you do that, you will be amazed at what will happen.

I see so many relationships that are destroyed, but through forgiveness and reconciliation, God is able to fix so many things. However, it will always cost you something. We are usually part of the problem. When we do not give up ourselves to God, the problem will never get better.

If you feel like you have failed or if you feel convicted, don't be embarrassed. When you read the Word of God and you realize that you missed the point, don't be embarrassed. Never be embarrassed by the Word of God when it sheds light on a portion of your heart where you need it to shine. God does not embarrass people.

Whenever God reveals something to you, He is more than capable of helping you overcome what He reveals. If you could fix the problem, it would have been fixed. That's why God is saying to come to Him: so that He can fix things as you abide in Him. There are some things that will only result in you abiding in Christ, in His Word, and allowing Him to work through you. Forgiveness and reconciliation are two of those things. Know that I am praying for you as you continue on this journey.

WORKBOOK

Chapter Ten Questions

Question: What principles of restoration can you learn from the story of Mephibosheth? What qualities in David led to his seeking out this restoration?

_____

_____

_____

_____

_____

_____

_____

_____

_____

_____

Question: *God has a way of working with what we can do and what we have, rather than focusing on what we don't have.* What resources do you have right now that you can use in obedience and faith?

_____

_____

_____

_____

_____

_____

_____

_____

_____

_____

_____

Question: What visible or obvious reminder of your past pain do you carry or encounter regularly, as Mephibosheth did with his lame feet? How can you turn this reminder of past pain into a reminder of God's gift of reconciliation and restoration?

_____

_____

_____

_____

_____

_____

_____

_____

_____

_____

_____

_____

Action: Read the story of Jesus and Peter, from Peter's denials to his meeting with the resurrected Jesus on the shore (Luke 22:31–34, 54–62; John 21). How did Jesus forgive Peter, reconcile with him, and then restore him to ministry?

_____

_____

_____

_____

_____

_____

_____

_____

_____

Chapter Ten Notes

_____

_____

_____

_____

_____

_____

_____

_____

_____

_____

_____

_____

_____

_____

_____

_____

_____

_____

_____

_____

_____

CONCLUSION

Freedom Through Forgiving

It is my sincere hope that, after having worked through this book, you better understand why it is so important to your spiritual growth that you learn to forgive and find joy in forgiving. Remember that, most of all, we forgive because God has called us to do so, and we long to please Him. However, there are numerous benefits to your walk with Christ as you learn to forgive. Releasing grudges you have been holding will allow you to enjoy a great freedom in Christ.

Remember what forgiveness is and what it is not, to make sure that you handle each situation appropriately. Don't allow yourself to be abused by others through premature reconciliation, but also, don't be abused by the enemy because you refuse to obey God's command to forgive. Above all, be prayerful, have a humble heart, and be guided by the amazing love of our Savior as you interact with others.

Forgiveness is a part of spiritual growth, and it is not a trivial matter. It is one of the things we do to become more

Christlike, and we rely on God's strength to carry us through. Just like with all issues of spiritual growth, at times you will struggle with forgiveness. You will make mistakes in the process of forgiveness, despite your best intentions. When you do, forgive yourself, and ask God to help you to do better next time, as you grow and learn.

I hope you will find the freedom that comes through living as a person who forgives others, and that you will become an agent of reconciliation in God's perfect timing. Being used by God in matters of reconciliation is a beautiful thing. I would like to end this book with a prayer for you and for all of us, as we work to be more like Jesus.

Pray this prayer with me:

> Father, thank You for this moment. Thank You for what You've done. Lord, we're always safer when we stand on Your Word. Your people have heard and listened. There's so much that's happening in our hearts. We pray, Lord, for the gift of forgiveness to be granted to each and every one of us. And we pray, Lord, for this diamond of redemption and reconciliation of relationships to be brought together, assisting You in this divine dream of reconciling humanity. We pray for those people to whom we need to extend the gift of reconciliation. We pray that You may set us free. We pray that You would help us to put on love, so that Your peace may rule our hearts. We pray that the Word of Christ may abide in us richly. And finally, we pray that You may give us the ability to live our lives as acts of worship to You. In Jesus' name, amen.

Notes

1. Williamson, Marianne. Quoted in Patrick Mabilog, "Forgiveness: Why Holding on to That Grudge Will Only Hurt You," *Christian Today,* March 2016. https://www.christiantoday.com/article/forgiveness-why-holding-onto-that-grudge-will-only-hurt-you/83008.htm.

2. Abraham Lincoln. Quoted in William Barclay, *More New Testament Words* (SCM Press Ltd., 1958).

3. Berman, Mark. "'I Forgive You.' Relatives of Charleston Church Shooting Victims Address Dylann Roof." *The Washington Post.* June 19, 2015. https://www.washingtonpost.com/news/post-nation/wp/2015/06/19/i-forgive-you-relatives-of-charleston-church-victims-address-dylann-roof/?noredirect=on&utm_term=.8bc2d0c31b5b.

4. White, Paula. *Deal With It!: You Cannot Conquer What You Will Not Confront.* Thomas Nelson, 2004.

5. Berg, Yehuda. Quoted in Stephanie Bennett Vogt, *A Year to Clear: A Daily Guide to Creating Spaciousness in Your Home and Heart* (Hierophant Publishing, 2015).

6. Eggerichs, Emerson. *Love and Respect.* HarperCollins, 2004.

7. Conwell, Russell Herman, and Robert Shackleton. *Acres of Diamonds.* Harper and Brothers, 1915.

About the Author

Mackenzie Kambizi is the senior pastor of Ethan Temple Seventh-day Adventist Church, which belongs to the Allegheny West Conference. He counts it an honor and privilege to pastor his divine assignment, to serve Jesus Christ, and to equip people for service.

Pastor Kambizi founded the "Truth for These Times" broadcast and functions as a speaker. He has served as a local and international evangelist in more than fifteen countries on four continents.

Pastor Kambizi delivers bold, thought-provoking preaching, creative teaching, resourceful training, and in-depth mentoring. He provides practical motivation through the relevant, biblically based approach of principle preaching.

A recipient of numerous awards, Pastor Kambizi is also known for his involvement in the community. He is a bold activist, which has led him to numerous city board memberships and an invitation to the U.S. Senate and U.S. House of Representatives.

Pastor Kambizi's vision and mission for ministry are to empower people to have a living relationship with God by increasing faith, instilling holiness, and inspiring hope.

A man devoted to his family, he is the father to Madison, Morgan, Unathi and Nkosi Mackenzie Chamu Jr.

About Sermon To Book

SermonToBook.com began with a simple belief: that sermons should be touching lives, *not* collecting dust. That's why we turn sermons into high-quality books that are accessible to people all over the globe.

Turning your sermon series into a book exposes more people to God's Word, better equips you for counseling, accelerates future sermon prep, adds credibility to your ministry, and even helps make ends meet during tight times.

John 21:25 tells us that the world itself couldn't contain the books that would be written about the work of Jesus Christ. Our mission is to try anyway. Because in heaven, there will no longer be a need for sermons or books. Our time is now.

If God so leads you, we'd love to work with you on your sermon or sermon series.

Visit www.sermontobook.com to learn more.

CPSIA information can be obtained
at www.ICGtesting.com
Printed in the USA
FSHW022023201220
77057FS